BECAUSE DONORS WANT TO SHARE

BECAUSE DONORS
WANT TO SHARE

A Donor-Centric Approach to Individual Fundraising

CARL W. DAVIS, CFRE

ISBN: 0692601325
ISBN 13: 9780692601327

THE INTRODUCTION

The American approach to philanthropy is rooted in our fundamental understanding of what it means to be a country of free citizens who are all equal before the law rather than the subjects of a monarch or the subservient minions of a dictator.

From time immemorial cultures have realized the need to take action for the social wellbeing of their societies. The old European approach to this topic was simply that the gentle-class of landed aristocrats would pay for things such as the arts, poor-relief, and the Church from the largess they accumulated through the feudalistic economic system that allowed that class to prosper so greatly while the majority of the population, who were peasants, remained impoverished and powerless. This system of patronage ensured that society had the institutions that the noble class wanted the society to have and that those institutions functioned in ways that were pleasing to the noble class. To a smaller extent, this approach of "patronage philanthropy" is still used in some places today.

Other cultures, in more recent times, have chosen to address issues of social need by turning to communism or socialism. These societies simply take resources from the pockets of their population through taxation and then hire government bureaucrats to dole some that money out according to their own will and pleasure in the name of improving society for everyone. Systems of this sort are notoriously inefficient, plagued with corruption, wasteful and unable to be held to account. Additionally, the priorities of the bureaucrats doling out the tax money often do not align with the real and felt needs of the population. These systems become little more than ways to enrich government bureaucrats and by extension their friends, drain resources from the population and leave the needs of society largely unmet.

The American way of addressing our social issues is different from either of those models in that in our country free citizens come together of their own volition and voluntarily form organizations to address the societal concerns about which they care. They use the structure of the corporation to accomplish this objective. The mission of these corporations is not to generate revenue for their owners, but rather to accomplish a goal related to social improvement. Our tax code has been designed to allow citizens to deduct the money they personally contribute to such organizations from their federal income tax liability. Additionally, the organizations themselves do not incur federal income tax liability for the income they receive from their donors. Thus, we call these organizations nonprofit, tax exempt corporations. Other citizens who share the goal of the nonprofit organization's founders also contribute to the organization from their personal resources and the nonprofit organization develops a donor base comprised of free individuals who choose to use their money to improve their society in ways that align with their values. If donors do not believe a particular nonprofit is effective, they will give to a different nonprofit that is designed to accomplish a similar goal more effectively. This free market system ensures efficiency and holds both the board members who run nonprofit organizations and the staff they hire to operate them to account.

Additionally, each citizen is free to choose which nonprofit(s) he or she will or will not support at any given time, reflecting respect for each citizen's private property rights and giving each citizen the opportunity to shape his or her community according to his or her own priorities, a role reserved only for the gentry in ancient times and to powerful government agents in communist or socialist nations today.

This book is designed to help the leaders of today's American nonprofit organizations engage and empower donors to accomplish their personal philanthropic goals, to the betterment of their communities, states, our nation and the world. This book is written because donors want to share.

CONTENTS

Chapter 1

※ ※ ※

DONOR-CENTRIC FUNDRAISING

"Lillian was a schoolteacher. She spent her entire life teaching first graders how to read. It makes sense that her IRA money gets used to promote literacy." Those are the words that Tom said to me over dinner on an October afternoon when he decided to make a major gift to the nonprofit for which I worked. I was the Development Officer privileged to help Tom honor his late wife with an IRA rollover gift made to our Endowment in her name. There are children in the world today who are able to read because Tom decided to honor Lillian by making a charitable gift with $100,000 from the IRA that he inherited from her.

Nonprofit organizations exist as conduits for charitable minded individuals to accomplish their personal philanthropic goals. In the example above, Tom wanted to carry on his late wife's legacy of helping young people become literate. He used the nonprofit I worked for to accomplish that goal by making a gift to our Endowment Fund and designating the annual earnings from that gift to support our work to increase literacy. My role as the gift officer was to identify Tom as a potential donor, get to know his philanthropic goal, and then to make sure he knew how he could achieve that goal through the nonprofit for which I worked. I also had to make sure Tom knew the different ways he could accomplish his goal. In this case it made the most sense for him to give money from an IRA that had belonged to his wife. His gift qualified as his required minimum distribution and he was able to reduce his tax burden by giving in that way. After I asked him to make the gift, I made sure he knew that his gift was appreciated and had the impact in the world he hoped for. My role as the Gift Officer was to help him accomplish his philanthropic goal efficiently. That is the role of the nonprofit development officer: to help donor's dreams come true.

This book is designed to present a donor-centric view of fundraising and give the reader proven techniques to raise funds in a donor-centric way. In the donor-centric view, nonprofit agencies never need to receive. Instead, donors want to share. Donors want to share their resources not with the accounts held by 501(c)(3) corporations but rather wish to use their resources to meet the needs they see in their world. Donors give to the need they want to meet. They give to make the world look the way they want it to look, to be the way they want it to be. Our nonprofit agencies exist as tools for donors to use to bring their dreams to fruition. It makes sense to call a nonprofit organization an agency because it is an agent of the donor's philanthropy. It is our privilege and pleasure as the staff and volunteers who work at those nonprofit agencies to help our donors make the world a better place.

A failure to view fundraising from a donor-centric perspective causes many people to be afraid of fundraising. People feel they will "bother their friends" if they ask them to make a gift to a nonprofit they care about. Others are afraid of offending people. Such fears come from a misunderstanding of fundraising. In order to help people who have such concerns understand the joy they can find in donor-centric fundraising I ask them to think about their favorite restaurant. Doubtless it is a place they love to go whenever possible. They must enjoy the food and they likely enjoy the ambience as well. Perhaps they know the chef, manager or other staff who work there. Almost all of us have at least one favorite restaurant. I then ask them a simple question: Have they ever invited someone else to eat at that restaurant? Of course they have! They were likely excited to do so because they wanted to invite a person they cared about to have the same good experience that they enjoy when they eat there. Asking someone else to give to a nonprofit we care about is no different. The analogy extends even further. We ask our friends to join us at our favorite restaurant because we want our friends to enjoy the food and environment. We don't ask them to dine with us at our favorite restaurant because we want the restaurant to meet its revenue target for that quarter. We are *diner-centric* not *restaurant-centric* when we invite our friends to join us for dinner just as we should be *donor-centric* and not *agency-centric* in our invitation to share a charitable gift. We also only invite our friends who we know will enjoy the offerings of our favorite restaurant to join us. We would not invite our vegetarian friends to join us at the steak house. We know our friends and we know the menu at the restaurant. When the two match up, we are excited to invite our friends to go to dinner with us without anxiety and we find that they are usually very happy, even excited, to accept our offer. Our friends will often even thank us for introducing them to a new restaurant that is likely to become one of their favorite places to eat as well. The donor-centric fundraiser is frequently thanked by the excited donors whom he or she has helped accomplish their philanthropic goal. Donor-centric fundraising is fun for all involved.

This book starts out by addressing Major Gifts. This is not because a nonprofit should begin its fundraising strategy by focusing on Major Gifts. As you will read in chapter seven, a nonprofit must have a healthy Annual Fund before it can launch a successful Major Gift program. The book starts by talking about Major Gifts because it is in working with Major Donors that the true nature of Donor-Centric fundraising is most clear, as in the example of Tom above. By properly understanding how Major Gifts are identified, cultivated, solicited and stewarded, the reader will gain a better appreciation for the importance of having an efficient donor-centric Annual Fund system. Additionally, if a donor reaches his or her full philanthropic potential, in most cases, he or she will ultimately make a Major or Planned Gift. Therefore it is our ultimate goal as fundraisers to have all of our donors eventually become Major Donors.

In Chapter Three we address Planned Gifts and some of the various methods that donors may use to make a Major Gift such as Bequests, Pledges, Gifts of Stock, Charitable Gift Annuities (CGA), Charitable Remainder Trusts (CRT), Charitable Lead Trusts (CLT), Gifts of Life Insurance and gifts made from a donor's Individual Retirement Account (IRA). The description of these gift types is intentionally brief as this book is not intended to be a technical manual of Planned Giving techniques. Instead the goal of this chapter is to give the new Major Gift Fundraiser a basic overview of some of the most common tools that his or her donors may use to accomplish their philanthropic goals and thereby be better equipped for donor-centric Major Gift work.

The fourth chapter covers fundraising campaigns because at some point almost every nonprofit decides to enter into a fundraising campaign. Some nonprofits design their entire fund development plan around their annual fund campaign. Other, typically larger, nonprofits will frequently have several different campaigns underway at the same time. Still other nonprofits only do campaigns for special projects such as capital needs or a Major Gifts initiative for a special philanthropic priority or to celebrate an important event in the life of that nonprofit such as an anniversary. Regardless of what type of campaign is being considered, there is the need for good planning and healthy goal setting. In this chapter we will explore how those two concepts are interrelated and essential for success. This chapter contains guidelines and formulas that can be used to form effective donor-centric campaign goals for any type of fundraising campaign, thus allowing the reader to design a donor-centric campaign that can be as successful as possible.

In some circles the word "Fundraiser" is considered a synonym for "Gala." Chapter Five is devoted to discussing fundraising events. In that chapter we will explore how some events are not donor-centric at all and should be removed from a well-run nonprofit's fundraising plan altogether and why other events should be included (even though they may cost the agency money) because they are donor-centric events that will ultimately empower our donors to better achieve their philanthropic goals. The purpose of this chapter is to encourage each nonprofit to stop doing fundraising events that are not donor-centric and start doing events that are donor-centric. The chapter provides examples of specific events that are in use in the nonprofit community today and shares examples of how events can be used in a donor-centric development plan to help donors have the impact in the world that they desire to have.

As we explore how to set a healthy campaign goal and ensure that all events our nonprofit hosts are donor-centric, it will become clear that the well-run nonprofit needs to accurately collect and effectively analyze certain points of data. The sixth chapter, entitled "Metrics" describes exactly what data a donor-centric fundraising department needs to collect and how that data should be measured and reported. It also gives some guidance on how the data should be analyzed to help Major Gift Officers be as effective as possible and gives specific real life examples of ways you can effectively communicate the work that your Development Department is doing to your board and executive leadership by presenting the data you collect and analyze to your agency's leadership in ways that will make sense to them and help your nonprofit effectively perform donor-centric fundraising in your annual fund using mail appeal, monthly recurring giving programs as well as in your Major and Planned Gift efforts.

In Chapter Seven, we take a deep look at the heart and soul of every well-run nonprofit's fundraising plan, the Annual Fund. The Annual Fund should provide funding for the base operations of your nonprofit. The reason for that is because the income your nonprofit receives from its annual fund donors is the most dependable income your agency has. It is the most dependable because it is the most diversified. Major Gifts rise out of a healthy annual fund. If the Annual Fund is healthy your agency will have major gift prospects. If your Annual Fund is not healthy it likely will not have true major gift prospects (donors who will make gifts to your nonprofit from their accumulated wealth instead of just from their income). Direct Mail, E-mail, Telephone Campaigns, Post Card Campaigns and Monthly Recurring Gift programs will all be explored in this chapter through the lens of donor-centricity. This chapter concludes by describing how you can identify Major and Planned Gift prospects from your annual fund, and in that sense this book comes full circle to the theme of chapter one – helping donors achieve their philanthropic goal in as powerful a way as possible.

Finally, Chapter Eight provides a simple collection of resources that the reader may find helpful in creating a donor-centric fundraising plan. The resources included in this section are: a Board Member Job Description and Commitment form, a sample Gift Acceptance Policy that will meet the needs of most small and medium sized nonprofits, A sample confidentiality policy that can be used by a nonprofit's staff and volunteers to ensure that donor information is treated properly by all who interact with that information while serving at the nonprofit.

Let us now begin this exploration of donor-centric individual fundraising by considering the Major Gift and the people who give them.

Chapter 2

MAJOR GIFTS

WHAT IS A MAJOR GIFT?

There are two approaches to defining the term "Major Gift." The first approach is the most common approach and can be viewed as the agency-centric definition. That is, a Major Gift is defined in terms of the receiving nonprofit agency's budget. Using this approach a small agency may say "for us a major gift is any gift more than $1,000 because only 20% of our gifts are more than $1,000." A larger agency may say "For us, a Major Gift is a gift of $50,000 or more because we do not have the staff power to pay individual attention to donors who make gifts of lesser value." For an agency's Major Gift initiative to succeed, an agency-centric definition is needed to effectively target the agency's limited staff resources towards the donors where their effort will have the greatest impact. A common definition for Major Gift to large nonprofits in 2015 is a single gift of $10,000 or more. This means that at those nonprofits a Major Gifts Officer is not actively identifying, cultivating, soliciting or stewarding gifts of less than $10,000. Instead, their staff colleagues in the Annual Fund department will do that work. However, when the Major Gifts Officer is interacting with the donor he or she should always bear in mind a donor-centric definition of Major Gift.

From a donor's perspective a Major Gift is a gift made from accumulated assets as opposed to income. Two things are obvious in this donor-centric definition. First, the actual cash value of the Major Gift will be different for each donor based on the donor's personal financial circumstances and second, every bequest must be viewed as a Major Gift under this definition. The third implication of a gift that is funded from a donor's accumulated assets that is not always as obvious to major gift fundraisers is that the donor is more likely to wish his or her Major Gift to go into an endowment rather than an operating budget. Think about it like this, since the donor has worked for years to accumulate the wealth he is now considering giving to charity, he would prefer that "long term money" to have a "long term charitable impact." The money is currently in the donor's long term savings/investment portfolio so it makes sense to move that money into the nonprofit's long term savings/investment portfolio. This alignment shows respect for the donor's hard work to earn the wealth he is being asked to give to charity. This is a reality that many small nonprofits fail to recognize and that failure results in many donors saying no to major gift asks from small nonprofits who want to take the donor's major gift and spend it in their annual operating budget as soon as it is received. This is a major reason why larger and more established institutions receive more Major Gifts than small operations do, because the larger agency can assure the donor that the donor's long term assets can have long term charitable impact through that nonprofit's endowment. A well run nonprofit meets its operating needs through its Annual Fund and solicits Major Gifts for special purposes that excite donors such as a special initiative or capital campaign and for the agency's endowment fund where the donor's long term accumulated assets can do long term charitable good.

WHY DO DONORS MAKE MAJOR GIFTS?

Ultimately donors make charitable gifts including Major Gifts because they have decided that giving that portion of their money to charity is their preferred use of the resource. The picture on this book's cover illustrates that point. In that picture a young boy is feeding his ice cream cone to his dog. The boy wears a smile on his face showing that his decision to share his ice cream with his dog instead of eating the dessert himself is giving him more joy than he would have experienced had he simply ate the ice cream. Donors make a major gift because they want to share. They find joy and satisfaction in the act of giving.

Major Gift Fundraising must be viewed from a donor-centric perspective. What motivates the donor to give the gift? Usually it is because the donor wants to see the world look a certain way and is willing to use his or her money to help make the world look that way. We call that having *interest* in the agency's mission. For instance, your donor may value a world where no child goes to sleep hungry. Your donor values that ideal so strongly that she is willing to give her money to buy food for hungry children. Your donor writes the check to your organization because she knows that your organization is doing good work to feed hungry children. Notice that the donor did not give because she cared that your agency's budget is balanced or because you were having a major gift campaign. The donor in that sense did not give TO your nonprofit organization, but rather THROUGH your nonprofit organization. Nonprofit organizations are best viewed as conduits of good work. Donors have the goal of improving their world in some specific way. They want to use their money to achieve that goal. They will use your nonprofit to achieve that goal with their money when they know that your nonprofit is doing the work it takes to make the world the way the donor wants the world to be and that you are doing that work well.

That is why it is very important to talk about the impact of your organization's work with your donors. Communicate to your donors how they have the power to make the world the way they want the world to be through their charitable giving. Share specific examples about how your agency is doing work that will make the world the way the donor wants the world to be (IE: better educated, healthier, fairer, more prosperous, etc.) Then invite the donor to take action to make the world the way the donor wants the world to be through a major gift to your nonprofit. Notice that I said invite the donor to achieve his or her goal THROUGH your nonprofit instead of making a gift TO your nonprofit. Appeal to the donor's desire instead of to your organization's needs. As gift officers we are inviting donors to provide education to children not to meet a campaign goal. We focus on the end result of the donor's charitable act because our organization is merely the conduit of the donor's goodwill.

I often say that my job as a Major Gifts Officer is to learn the philanthropic goals of my donor as they relate to my nonprofit. After I learn this, my goal is to help the donor develop a plan to accomplish his or her philanthropic goals by making a major gift.

In this regard, Major Gift Fundraisers are like matchmakers. We need to know our donors well, and we need to know the good work that our agency is doing well. We also need to know all of the various ways our donors can use their resources to accomplish their goals through our organization. We listen to our donors' philanthropic desires and dreams. We communicate with our donors about the work our nonprofit is doing that aligns with their expressed philanthropic goals. We match up the donor's desire with our agency's work and help the donor understand how he or she can have the impact he or she wants to have by making a major or planned gift.

The next function of the Major Gift Fundraiser is helping the donor make an informed choice about how they should best make their gift. Donors need to understand that they have many options about how they can make a major gift beyond simply writing a check. The options a specific donor has will depend on the laws of the country and state where that the donor lives as well as on the gift acceptance policy of the nonprofit to which the gift is being made. A function of the Major Gifts Officer is to make sure the donor knows all of the appropriate options available to him or her so that the donor can then speak with his or her personal legal/tax/financial expert(s) and make the best choice possible. Let me be clear, it is not the role of the Gift Officer to give legal, tax or financial advice to donors. In fact, Gift Officers must go out of their way to ensure the donor understands that the Gift Officer is not providing such guidance to the donor. That said, it is the job of the Major Gift officer to put various options on the donor's RADAR so that the donor can make the best, most informed decision possible. In order for the Major Gift Officer to be most effective he or she will need to have a functional understanding to the different ways a donor can make a major gift.

MAJOR GIFT FUNDRAISING PROCESS OVERVIEW

Major Gift Fundraising works on the same four stage donor cycle that all fundraising for nonprofits operates upon. The main difference is that in major gift fundraising, the donor leads the speed at which he or she moves through the cycle to a greater extent than the donor does in the Annual Fund fundraising system.

The four stages of the fundraising process are generally understood to be: **1. Identification 2. Cultivation 3. Solicitation and 4. Stewardship**.

In Annual Fund fundraising, stage one may be as simple as buying a mailing list of possible donors from a bulk mail company or (more productively) simply considering everyone in your current database as a prospect just because you have their contact information. The name of the game in the identification stage for Annual Fund fundraising is to cast a wide net. You want to send letters to as many people as your budget will allow. Cultivation for these donors may consist of simply sending the donor a copy of your newsletter. Solicitation likely means sending the donor an appeal letter and the stewardship stage may be accomplished by sending the donor a thank you note after the gift is received. The timing of those acts are controlled by your agency's mailing schedule and are designed to ensure that your agency gets the gifts it needs to fund its annual budget at the correct time each year. That is why this is fundraising effort is called the "Annual Fund." By its nature the system of the Annual Fund is very agency-centric even though good Annual Fund messaging must be as donor-centric as possible. This agency-centric schedule of a donor-centric message is appropriate for Annual Fund fundraising where gifts tend to be smaller, generally made from disposable income instead of accumulated assets, and are needed promptly for the agency's operating budget. However, we must take a different approach in raising Major Gifts.

In Major Gifts Fundraising each of the steps in the four stage fundraising process is personalized for the specific donor in question and we do not move from one step to the next simply because time has passed. We only move to the next step when we believe the donor is ready to move to the next step. Unlike in Annual Fund fundraising where the messaging is donor-centric but the system is agency-centric, in Major Gift Fundraising both the messaging and the system are as donor-centric as possible. We move at the donor's pace to accomplish the donor's philanthropic goals. This is another reason why agencies that raise Major Gifts to support special projects, campaigns or endowments are more successful than agencies who try to raise Major Gifts to support their operating budget. Special gifts and endowment fund gifts can progress at the donor's speed and need not be rushed like annual operating fund gifts need to be. This is also why intentional Major Gift efforts like Capital Campaigns take a very long time to execute.

Let us now look at each of the four fundraising stages through the lens of a Major Gift Fundraiser. A mature nonprofit with a healthy Major Gifts Fundraising plan will have several donors in each of these stages at any given time as illustrated in the chapter of this book called "Metrics." A newer or smaller nonprofit may find that all of their major gift prospects are still in the early stages of the process. The first stage or step in Major Gift fundraising is Identification.

MAJOR GIFT FUNDRAISING STEP ONE: IDENTIFICATION

Identifying the donors we will work with to raise Major Gift support is one of the most important steps in the fundraising process because if we identify good prospects, all of the other stages will be much easier than if we start our work with poor prospects. We therefore want to do as good of job as possible in identifying Major Gift prospects. Do not rush though this step. Do it thoroughly. Some nonprofits find that a good way to identify major gift prospects is to assemble a small group of volunteers who know the agency's donor base well and know the prospective donors from different perspectives and then have that small group brain storm a list of Major Gift Prospects together based on their personal knowledge of the donors in that agency's donor base. If this method is used, it is important for each person in the brainstorming group to understand the importance of confidentiality and to sign a confidentiality agreement prior to participating in the group. A sample confidentiality agreement is contained in Chapter Eight. The group should start their meeting my reviewing the Association of Fundraising Professional's publication entitled "A Donor's Bill of Rights" and understand that the information that they will learn about the agency's donors must not be used for any purpose except fundraising for that agency at that time. Other Major Gift Fundraisers prefer to perform this stage of the fundraising process in private after reviewing giving history reports or simply thinking about the people they personally know.

Whatever method is used to identify Major Gift prospects, it is important to realize that every Major Gift donor has three common traits. First, the donor has the **ABILITY** to make a Major Gift. Second, the donor has an **INTEREST** in your agency's mission. Third the donor has personal **LINKAGE** to your agency. Consider, for instance, a donor who just gave $50,000 to his local homeless shelter. He had ability (after all, he wrote the check). He also had an interest in helping the homeless. You know this because he could have given that check to the humane society, but instead he chose to give his gift of $50,000 to the homeless shelter because that is the agency whose mission interested him. Third, he gave to that specific homeless shelter as opposed to a different homeless program because he had some link to that nonprofit. At the very least, his linkage consisted of knowing that the agency existed. More likely he personally knew of its good work and believed that specific agency was well run. By looking at that simple example we see that the Major Gift Donor had **ABILITY, INTEREST** and **LINKAGE**. Every Major Gift donor shares those three traits. Think about your current donors and you will find this to be true without exception.

In the identification stage of Major Gift Fundraising we want to find donors who have high levels of Ability, Interest and Linkage. Of course, if a donor had high levels of all three of those metrics he or she would already be making large gifts to your agency. Therefore a great place to start looking for new major gift prospects is among your current high-level donors. Look at people who regularly give to the Annual Fund. Look at people who have given large or Major Gifts in the past. But also look for people who may be high in one or two of the areas but not all three. Finding people like this is the key to generating new Major Gift Donors. Your work with such donors is to raise the lowest of their three metrics to the next level through good cultivation. This will result in those donors making gifts of increased size. This is the heart and soul of a Major Gift Officer's work.

A donor's giving will never rise above the lowest of those three metrics. He may have high ability and high interest but low linkage to your agency. Therefore, he will not give a Major Gift to your agency because he doesn't know much about you. Another donor may have high ability and high linkage but doesn't really believe in your cause. She will not make a major gift to your agency either. In those cases it is your job to raise that lowest bar to the next level through cultivation. But what about the donor who has high interest and high linkage but does not have high ability in our estimation? Sadly, many major gift efforts overlook these donors as "unqualified prospects." I think that is a grave error and personally find that those donors are especially fun to work with because we gift officers are usually in the position of helping them realize a dream they thought impossible. These donors are our best candidates for large bequests or life income agreements. Remember, we said above that when using the donor-centric definition of Major Gift all bequests are Major Gifts because by definition they are made from the donor's accumulated assets. Therefore we need to treat bequest prospects like the Major Gift prospects that they are.

Another note, any donor with high interest and high linkage is worth exploring as a major gift prospect for the simple reason that we never truly know the financial ability of another person. We have all read stories about the preverbal millionaire next door who everyone thought was poor because he lived a frugal life. Of the three metrics, the one I care the least about is ability. Why is that? First, I should devote the least amount of my energy to it because it is the metric over which I have the least control. I can do much to raise a donor's linkage to my agency and I can even help raise a donor's interest in my agency's mission through education but there is not much I can do to raise a donor's ability. Therefore I don't spend much time focusing on it. I'd rather focus my energy on the metrics where my energy can have more impact and make a bigger difference. When in doubt, I simply assume that ability is present and cultivate the donor by paying attention to the donor's interest and linkage and working to improve those metrics through cultivation. More importantly, I don't worry too much about ability because as mentioned above, almost anyone has the ability to make a major gift via bequest and if the donor is truly interested in our mission and passionately linked to our agency we can likely figure out a way to make that donor's philanthropic dream come true using one of the many major gift tools we have at our disposal through Planned Giving. Those tools will be discussed in the part of this book that addresses Planned Giving. For now, just don't worry too much about ability. It must be said that this is also an area where many small nonprofits fail. Many times the board chair or executive director will come into the development director's office and hand her a copy of the latest newspaper article listing the ten richest people in America and say "Go get a major gift from one of these guys!" Of course, we know how that usually works. Much effort is wasted trying to get an appointment with someone who has little interest in the agency's mission and has no linkage to the agency. Even if a meeting is secured, it usually goes nowhere and everyone in the process feels like a failure. Ability alone does not make a Major Donor. Ability must be coupled with Interest and Linkage. A wise mentor of mine once described the Major Donor Identification Process by saying "I'm not looking for rich person. I'm looking for a generous person." That is true, and I would add it also takes caring about your agency's mission and knowing that your agency is effectively accomplishing your mission through well performed work for that generous person to make a Major Gift to your agency.

To identify Major Gift prospects considering Ability, Interest and Linkage start by making a list of the names of prospective Major Gift Donors for your nonprofit. Then rate each one as either: High, Medium, Low or Unknown in the areas of **Ability, Interest** and **Linkage**. I use a chart like the one below for this purpose.

To qualify as a legitimate prospect for a Major Gift the donor must score high in at least one, preferably two, of the three areas remembering that the least important of these three areas is ability.

Donor Name	Ability	Interest	Linkage
Jane Smith	Med	High	High
Bill Jones	High	?	High
Randy Johnson	High	Medium	Low

How many donors should you identify at one time? The answer to that question depends on who you are. A full time Major Gifts Officer at a large established nonprofit who is experienced, well trained and has no other professional duties except to raise Major Gifts generally manages a portfolio of between 100 to 200 donors. I have found that number can be higher when working with membership based nonprofits because those donors build their linkage and interest faster than donors to non-membership based nonprofits simply by virtue of participating in the membership activities of the agency. When working with donors who are actually members of the nonprofit I serve, I am comfortable with a portfolio of up to 350 donors at a time. Ideally those donors are equally spread through the four stages of the fundraising process. A small nonprofit with only one development officer who is responsible for all areas of fundraising or an agency where the Executive Director serves as chief cook and bottle washer may have 5 to 10 Major Donors in total. While there is no uniform answer to this question, I wish to highlight this next point as strongly as I possibly can. **Volunteers who are working to raise Major Gifts are shown to be most effective when they have only three to five prospects.** When I train volunteers to raise Major Gifts, I ask each of them to identify only three names. The point here is to focus on quality over quantity. Also, studies have shown that when a volunteer has more than five prospects the volunteer often feels pressured and may rush "to get through the list." Also, for volunteers with other obligations such as professional, personal and family commitments, managing a major gift portfolio of more than 5 donors can prove to be too much work. It may stop being fun at that point. Successful major gift fundraising is fun for all involved. After all, we are making the world a better place and helping donors realize their philanthropic dreams. It is fun and exciting work in which to be involved! Even volunteers with the best of intentions may find that the task is too great and the quality of their work may not be what they wish it was if they try to handle too many donors at once. It is better to simply work on three names at a time and do the work well instead of starting with a large list and doing the work less than well. After your prospects have been identified and ranked based on their Ability, Interest and Linkage, the next step is cultivation.

MAJOR GIFT FUNDRAISING STEP TWO: CULTIVATION

Now that you have a list of prospects and have rated each one on the metrics of **Ability, Interest** and **Linkage** it is time to start cultivating them as Major Gift Prospects. Because Major Gift fundraising is donor-centric you must create a custom plan for each donor based on that donor's unique needs and interests. Remember that the lowest of their three metrics (**Ability, Interest, Linkage**) is what is capping their giving at its current level. The ultimate goal of cultivation is to raise that lowest metric to its next level, thus lifting the cap that is keeping the donor's giving at its current level and thereby securing the Major Gift that will accomplish the donor's philanthropic goal.

The first step in the cultivation process is to communicate with the donor and confirm or correct your initial ratings. Generally this is best done face-to-face via informal conversation. You need to get to know the donor better. Specifically, you want to learn more about the donor's passion for your agency's mission and his or her linkage or connection to your agency. This involves much listening to what your donor is saying with his or her words and his or her actions.

During the cultivation process you want to communicate two realities to your donor. The first is that your agency is doing good work that your donor cares about. The second is that your agency is doing that good work well. Stories often best communicate these points. Tell your donor stories. Share examples of the work your agency is doing that aligns with the donor's charitable interest. Share examples of how your agency is effective thus showing your donor that you do your good work well. There is certainly a place for sharing the results of an audit or your rating from Charity Navigator with your donor during cultivation but the lion's share of your work to communicate that your agency is doing good work and is doing it well should be communicated via interesting and exciting stories that help the donor emotionally and cognitively experience your agency's impact on the philanthropic priority that the donor cares about.

It is important to note that the individual techniques used to effectively cultivate donors and the speed at which the process will move is heavily dependent upon the donor's culture. Cultural norms around these practices vary greatly within the United States. The good Gift Officer must be able to adapt to the preferred style of the donor. Over the years I have worked across the United States and these days work primarily in the Southern United States where I find the style of most donors closely matches my preferred personal style of interpersonal communication. It is important to be sensitive to the donor's sense of propriety throughout the cultivation process. For instance, when I used to work with attorneys in large Northern cities, I quickly learned that they usually valued very succinct and quick communications and they generally preferred e-mail over telephone calls. That communication style would be considered rude by other donors I have worked with in other parts of the country where personal phone calls are preferred over e-mail and each call begins with a polite conversation about how the other person is doing that day, what the weather is like near them and other general pleasantries before the actual reason for the phone call is brought up. The good Gift Officer knows the style of communication his or her donors prefer and tailors his or her communication style to meet the expectations and needs of the donor.

A common question is "How do I secure a face-to-face meeting with a person I have identified as a Major Gift Prospect?" If the person is someone you see frequently and interact with casually, you may simply choose to take advantage of one of your frequent routine meetings with that person to have a conversation about that person's philanthropic interests and your nonprofit's work. This is the most common approach for volunteer fundraisers who are friends with their Major Gift prospects. When I approach perspective donors as a professional Major Gifts Officer, I usually do so with a letter to them introducing myself as the Major Gifts Officer for my nonprofit. I send such letters to every donor who has a strong history of giving to my nonprofit but has not yet made a Major Gift and to donors who have made a Major Gift or bequest in the past but are not currently in my portfolio of active prospects because their gift was made many years ago. This is my preferred method for new Major Gift prospect acquisition. In the letter I thank the donor for his or her strong history of giving to our work over the past years. I explain that I will be in the donor's geographic area during a certain range of dates and would enjoy the opportunity to meet together to thank him or her in person for his or her past support, answer any questions he or she may have about the impact that his or her past gifts have had and most importantly to learn more about the donor and his or her philanthropic priorities. The letter provides the donor with my contact information and invites the donor to contact me if they would like to schedule a meeting. I usually send the letters about one month before I will be in their geographic area. Personally, I find that about 10% of those letters result in a donor contacting me to schedule a one-on-one meeting. The donor will naturally contact me with their preferred method of communication. That tells me much about how the donor prefers to be contacted. If the donor calls me on the phone, I know the donor likes phone calls. If the donor e-mails or writes, I know the donor would prefer that I reach out to him or her in that way. I find this to be a good practice because all Major Gift prospects are given a personal touch from the Gift Officer and they are able to opt in to a Major Gift conversation by replying to the Gift Officer's letter. Using this method I only meet with people who obviously want to meet with me since they called or e-mailed me to schedule the visit. It also gives every donor I have identified as a prospect the option of meeting with me, so prospects will not feel left out because they were not selected for a donor visit when their neighbor was.

What about people who have not yet made a gift to your nonprofit? How do you approach them for a Major Gift conversation? Frankly, people with no giving history to my nonprofit are not likely to make my RADAR as a Major Gift prospect. I let them respond to some Annual Fund appeals first and only qualify them as a Major Gift Prospect after they have taken the step of giving a gift in response to an Annual Fund ask. Even for very wealthy donors, the first gift to a new charity is not usually a Major Gift because although their ability may be high, their interest and or linkage are not yet high. We need to develop a relationship with them through the four stage donor cycle to raise their linkage and interest before they are approached for a major gift and in a healthy system that usually starts with a relatively small gift to the Annual Fund. There are exceptions to that rule and I have received Major Gifts from people with no prior giving history, but I would not design a Major Gift campaign based on raising Major Gifts from people with no giving history. If a donor is that motivated to make a Major Gift, the donor will come onto the RADAR of any Major Gift Officer who is doing his or her job without the Gift Officer needing to work hard to identify the donor. These are the people who call the Major Gift Officer and introduce themselves not the people that the Major Gift Officer needs to design a strategy to secure a first meeting with.

Let us consider how we would cultivate a donor we believe has high ability, low interest and moderate linkage. This tends to be a very common rating for potential major donors for agencies that are just starting their major gift efforts. Such a donor is basically a person who knows the agency a little bit; who is thought to have financial ability, and who is not necessarily passionate about the agency's mission but is certainly is not opposed to the mission. That is why he was rated high in ability, low in interest and moderate in linkage. Donors with this rating may respond best to cultivation from a personal friend who is involved with the nonprofit instead of from an employee of the nonprofit because the friend brings added linkage to the donor by virtue of his or her personal relationship with the donor and his or her connection to the nonprofit. To reach donors like this as effectively as possible it is important that the nonprofit's professional staff and volunteer fundraisers work closely together as a team. In the case of this example since the lowest of those three metrics is the donor's interest in the agency's mission the main goal of the cultivation plan should be to raise his interest in the mission work. This is usually best accomplished through education about the ways that the agency is making the world better. Sometimes we need to start off by making sure our donor knows that there is a problem in our world and that our agency is working to solve that problem. For the case of this example let us imagine that your agency's mission is to mentor fatherless boys in your community and that you have a social relationship with the donor. He knows about your volunteer work at the agency where you are now volunteering to raise Major Gifts. In this case you might want to simply meet your perspective donor for a friendly visit over coffee and tell him about your recent experience mentoring a young man who lacks a father figure. Tell him how rewarding you find your volunteer work and how you see the impact of your work in the improved lives of the young people your agency helps. Be sure to listen to the perspective donor more than you talk during your meeting. Answer any questions he has. Make him feel heard not lectured to. The goal of that cultivation visit is simply to share your story and see how the donor reacts. You want him to leave that meeting thinking that your agency is making the world better and maybe even more importantly that you cared about his feelings and thoughts on the topic. This communicates to your donor that your agency is meeting a need in the world and that he can be part of meeting that need as well. That meeting's goal is to increase his interest in the work your agency does so that accomplishing that work will become one of the donor's philanthropic priorities. Most likely he will think the work you are doing is great and tell you that he is glad that your community has a program like the one you volunteer with. That evening or the next day you might want to e-mail him a link to your agency's webpage that contains a video about your agency's work and say "When we had coffee you mentioned you liked the work that we are doing to help our community's at-risk kids. I thought you would love seeing this video. It really gives me hope when I watch it." You have now had two cultivation actions with this donor. Ideally you will record these actions in your database, or at least in a spreadsheet or on a file card. If you are a professional fundraiser you must record these actions in your computerized database. If you are a volunteer, it is highly encouraged that you make notes and share them with your agency's staff so they can be added to the individual donor's database record. Pay attention to how the donor responds to your actions. Answer any questions he has promptly. The next time your agency has an open house or a cocktail hour, invite your prospect to join you at that event as your guest. That will not only give him a chance to see how your agency is making his community better (increasing his interest) but also increase his second lowest metric, linkage by connecting him to other people in the agency in addition to yourself. This takes time. It moves at the donor's pace. If the donor is Johnny-on-the-spot with questions and always wants to know more right away then you need to be quick with your responses to him. If the donor is not that fast, then you must be patient. Maybe he did not answer the e-mail you sent about the video. The next time you see him you tell him another story about a different boy you have seen your agency help. Remember our goal is to help the donor accomplish his philanthropic goal and allow the donor to make an informed choice about how he wants to do that. It may be that the donor will not develop an interest in your agency to a level high enough to make a major gift. That is okay. Remember your goal here is donor-centric. You are working to help this donor accomplish his or her philanthropic goal. If you have educated the donor enough about your mission and at that point the donor decides he still shows no interest, you have done your job. Let's be honest, each of us could think of several charitable causes that we would never give our money to because those causes do not align with our values. There is nothing wrong with this. Each person has the right to choose which causes they support and which causes they choose not to support. Sometimes, in cultivation we realize that the prospective donor we are working with is not going to choose our nonprofit's work as part of his or her philanthropic priorities. If you come to that conclusion while working with a donor during cultivation it is time to move on to a different donor in a polite and respectful way. You should invest your time and energy with donors where it will have more impact. In most cases however the donor's interest will increase through good cultivation. Back to our example, perhaps in the course of your conversation your donor has mentioned to you how lucky he feels that he had a good father unlike the boys in your program who are fatherless. That is important information, be sure to note it in your database. It is impossible to know when the cultivation stage will end with a particular donor just by reading a book or article about the topic. Each situation is unique and very donor specific. However, when you have done enough cultivation asking for the gift will feel natural and it will be fun. If you don't feel comfortable asking the donor if he would like to join you in supporting your program with a major gift then it is a good sign that you need to do more cultivation. I have seen cultivation move so fast that the donor is ready to make a major gift the day after the first visit. I have also seen it take several years. The correct pace for major gift cultivation is the pace that the donor feels comfortable with. When you believe that the donor's lowest level metric has been raised to the next level, it is time for the next step in the fundraising process; solicitation. You will often know that you are getting close to solicitation time because the donor will start to talk with you about the idea of making a charitable gift. This is a great sign that you have done cultivation well. You have raised that lowest metric and now the next gift is on the horizon. In most cases though, you will need to be the one to bring up the topic of the major gift with the donor.

MAJOR GIFT FUNDRAISING STEP THREE: SOLICITATION

This is the step of fundraising that most people think of when they hear the word "fundraising." Similarly, many people wrongly think that all Major Gift Officers do is go around asking people for money. Those misconceptions come from a failure to view fundraising as a four step process of which solicitation is the smallest and shortest step. Each step of the four stage process is equally "fundraising." A healthy fund raising professional manages relationships with donors through all of these stages.

One of the most common mistakes that new fundraisers make is rushing through cultivation to get to solicitation because there is a motivation, either external (from an executive director who does not understand the process) or internally (from a desire to "close a gift"). Such rushing also comes from a failure to understand the proper place for solicitation in the four stage donor cycle. One time, many years ago, I was meeting with a donor and a brand new fundraising colleague was with me as part of his training. The three of us met at a restaurant that the donor had suggested. It was near the donor's office and had the advantage of having a private room where the three of us were seated to eat our lunch. It was my first visit with the donor so my goal was simply to get to know him and do my best to make him feel appreciated for the gifts he had given to my agency over the past years. To my horror, after the dishes were cleared by the waitress my new colleague brushed the remaining silverware aside with his arm, leaned over the table, looked the donor in the eye and said "Okay, let's cut the bullshit. What are you going to give to (name of the agency I worked for at that time) this year?" I will not give you the details of the rest of that meeting. I will say we never received a gift from that donor again. I also became very gun shy about allowing new gift officers to come with me on donor visits. That is certainly an extreme case, but many gift officers rush to solicitation too fast, albeit in a more tactful fashion than my former colleague.

When cultivation is done well, solicitation naturally happens. To illustrate, let us consider the analogy of a car's transmission. In the case of an automatic transmission, a car will automatically shift in to the higher gear as the driver accelerates. On a car with a manual transmission, there will come a point where the engine cannot make the car go any faster unless the gear is shifted. It is clear to the driver that it is time to shift gears by looking at the car's tachometer and by feeling how the responsiveness of the car has changed as the RPM's have increased. Just as the driver of a car will know when to shift gears, the Gift Officer and the donor will know it is time for the gift to be made because the donor will feel his philanthropic goals are not advancing at the speed he would like. When a donor senses this before the Gift Officer, the donor may make the major gift before even being "formally asked" to make the gift, just as a car with an automatic transmission will shift gears when the car needs to shift gears to respond to the desire of the driver to go faster. I say that to illustrate the point that if a Gift Officer does a good job of cultivation, eventually the donor will make a gift without being asked (in most cases). Ok, you say, then why bother with solicitation? Why not just cultivate, cultivate, cultivate and let the gifts roll in? The answer to that question is that the donor is not an automatic transmission that will always shift at the best time and into the correct gear. The donor may not make the best gift possible to accomplish his or her philanthropic goal in the best way possible. In other words, the donor may make a gift that would not accomplish his or her philanthropic goal as well as a different gift might. The job of the Major Gift Officer during Cultivation is to learn the donor's philanthropic goals so that during solicitation the Major Gift Officer can propose a gift idea that accomplishes the donor's goals as much as possible. For instance, let's suppose a certain charity allows donors to create a Named Fund within its endowment in the name of a donor's loved one for a gift of $30,000 or more. The donor, who has been cultivated well but not solicited, may decide to make a gift of $25,000 tomorrow just because he loves the nonprofit's work so much that he wants to share a gift to help accomplish its mission. Because cultivation has been so successful the donor just mails his check to the agency where it is received and put into the agency's annual fund. The Gift Officer in that situation failed the donor by not soliciting soon enough. Before the donor made his gift of $25,000 to the annual fund, the donor should have been informed that for $30,000 to the agency's Endowment he could have created a fund named in honor of his loved one. How do you think that donor will feel when he learns that for $5,000 more he could have honored a person he loves with a legacy fund but no one ever told him that until after his money was spent? Had the Gift Officer solicited sooner, he could have informed the donor of all of the donor's options so the donor could make the best possible choice to accomplish his philanthropic goal in the way that was best for the donor. That is being donor-centric. Obviously, we never want our donors to feel disappointed with their charitable giving. We want donors to feel good about the informed choice they made to accomplish their philanthropic goal. We solicit specific gifts because we want donors to accomplish their specific goals.

Returning to the example about cultivating a major gift for a nonprofit that helps at-risk boys, if you as the fundraiser felt that it was now time to ask your donor for a major gift to your program for at-risk boys you might say something like "Dave, you know that the at-risk boys program is something I really care about. I know from our conversations over the past months that you share that value with me. I want you to know about an option that the boy's program has. We have an endowment fund that provides the financial support to help the boys we work with and we have naming opportunities for donors make major gifts. You said several times how great your dad was and how lucky you feel to have had him in your life. For a gift of $25,000 you can create an endowed fund in your dad's name that will fund a mentor for a boy who didn't have a dad like you did every year in your dad's name. It is a great way to do good in our world and honor your dad. Is that something you would be interested in?"

After asking that question, be quiet and let the donor answer. There is no wrong answer. Because this is a donor centric question only the donor can know what the right answer will be for him. Our job is to present the donor with an option so that he can make an informed choice about fulfilling his philanthropic goal. Let us go through a few possible answers to that question and discuss what our response might be to his answer.

Possible Answer One: "Yes. That sounds very interesting to me. How can I do that?" The first words said to that donor must be "thank you." Communicate that the donor's decision is exciting and is going to have a strong impact. He just made the world a better place by making the choice he made. Then discuss logistical details. Explain the ways he might want to fund his gift (appreciated stock vs. cash) and agree upon a next step to take place as soon as possible. IE: give the donor the self-addressed stamped envelope you brought to the meeting in anticipation of his decision so he can just write a check and mail it to your agency's office as easily as possible. Or give him the paper with your agency's stock broker's information so he can transfer the stock. Tell him you will call him as soon as the gift arrives to confirm it has arrived and then discuss how to recognize him for this gift. Explain that he will now be invited to the agency's annual donor dinner that fall that his gift will be listed in the annual report unless he would prefer anonymity, etc. Thank him again and again. Follow up with a thank you letter from you and an official thank you from the agency. In short, you have already moved to the next step of the fundraising process; steward-ship. If you are a volunteer working with a staff partner on this gift, your answer may simply be "Thanks, Dave! I'm so excited you are going to do this. Our Development Officer, Nicole Hamilton will call you to-morrow to discuss the details. What is a good number for her to reach you at and what time of day should she call?"

There are other possible answers that the perspective donor might give. Here are a few possibilities and some thoughts about how the Major Gift fundraiser might reply to them.

Possible Answer Two: "That is interesting to me but not some-thing I'm prepared to do at this time." Your response might be "I understand. It is a great program and an option you might want to consider is creating that fund I mentioned with a bequest in your estate plans. It is not something that needs to be funded right away. Many people make our agency the beneficiary of part of their life insurance policy, retirement account or a beneficiary in their will. That way they make supporting the kids in our community part of their legacy. Here is some information about how to do that and how to ensure that your gift would create a fund to honor your dad if you wanted to set it up that way." In this case you have learned additional information from the donor's answer. You know that he is interested in making the gift you asked for but the timing is not right. The bequest is a tool that takes timing out of the equation and is therefore a tool you can use to help this donor accomplish his goal. In this case I would give him the bequest information and then the next time we met I would ask him if he had a chance to look it over and ask him what he thought of that option. Again, if you are a volunteer you may simply say, "Would it be okay if our development officer talked with you about how you could accomplish this goal through your estate plans?" instead of personally describing how that can be accomplished. This is an example of where good teamwork yields great results. The volunteer can approach the prospect he knows, and then the development officer can provide the donor with options to accomplish his goal that were not previously on the donor's RADAR.

Possible Answer Three: "I need to discuss that with my wife." Your answer might be something like "I think that is a great idea. Why don't you bring her to our next open house so she can see the program like you have." You have now learned that this couple makes their major gift decisions together and you need to involve the donor's wife in the cultivation process as well. You want to develop a cultivation plan for her just like you did for the donor. Since the donor you have been working with has greater linkage to your agency than his wife does, you should first begin by establishing linkage between the donor's wife and the agency, thus invite her to the next open house your agency hosts.

<u>Possible Answer Four:</u> "No, that is not something that interests me at this time." Something to note is that generally a donor doesn't just say "no." Usually the donor will tell you WHY he is not interested. You can then respond to the why. You do not respond to the why with the goal of changing the donor's mind. Instead you respond in a donor-centric fashion by affirming that you understand and respect the donor's decision. You use good communication skills to help the donor feel that he has been heard and is appreciated. I will often say something to the effect of "If you know of anyone else who you think might like to make an endowed gift like we discussed, please tell them about the program." Usually donors say that they will gladly do that and it helps everyone to feel good about the situation. In the rare case that the donor did just say "no" an appropriate response is "I certainly understand and respect that decision. If you ever change your mind, just let me know." In that case you do not keep cultivating the donor. You respect his answer and move your cultivation efforts to a different prospect whose interest and linkage may align better with your non-profit. However, if the donor tells you the reason he is saying no be sure to take note of it. If it is because of a circumstance that might change, keep track of that and when that circumstance changes it is okay to ask again. For instance, a donor may say "Right now my son just started college so I am not making any large charitable gifts until his college is paid for." The logical plan would be to keep in touch with that donor over the next four years. Make sure he gets your agency's newsletters and annual reports. Keep meeting him and sharing stories. Keep cultivating him over the years that his son is in school, build his interest and linkage as high as possible during that time then after the son is done with school ask the donor again.

Something to pay attention to, if the donor raises a serious objection about your agency's work at this time it is important to take note of this objection. Remember, that the thing that is stopping this donor from giving is likely stopping other donors from giving as well. This information is valuable to your agency and can be used to fix the problem in question if the concern is real or improve the agency's communication plan so that false negative impressions of your agency can be corrected. Individual Major Gift Donors are often the agency's first warning sign about a problem at the agency. This is logical but often overlooked. The people who are usually closest to the agency (thanks to our work to build strong linkage with them) are our major gift donors. Therefore they often spot problems first. Also, because we are asking our major gift donors to make very generous gifts of their hard earned resources their decision to say no to that request may be the first sign that trouble is brewing. A donor may be willing to give $100 without asking too many questions but a donor will not likely give $100,000 without exploring the agency's health more closely. In that regard Major Gift donors can be the proverbial canary in the coal mine. If many major gift asks are failing because donors are citing the same problem with the agency, it is a good sign that the problem is serious and needs to be addressed right away or eventually all donors will stop giving as time passes and the problem becomes apparent not only to those who are closest to the agency and inspecting it under the strictest scrutiny but also to the general donor base of the agency's Annual Fund. For this reason, well run agencies take feedback from their major donors as relayed through the agency's Major Gifts officers very seriously. A well run and healthy agency will find that most of its Major Gift asks end in yes.

Sometimes a donor says yes but then it takes a long time for the gift to actually arrive at your nonprofit. That is okay. Remember, we are moving at the donor's pace in Major Gift fundraising. It is important to keep in touch with that donor and ensure that any questions the donor has are answered accurately and promptly. Sometimes large gifts can be very complex and take time to be structured. Perhaps a donor has to liquidate or transfer an asset in order for the gift to happen or perhaps he needs to see his attorney and his CPA and their schedules are busy. Major Donors tend to be very busy people because they care about having an impact in the world (if they did not, they would not make a Major Gift). The important thing is to stay in good communication with your donor at all times, but especially at the time between when the donor said yes to your ask and when the gift has arrived at your nonprofit.

MAJOR GIFT FUNDRAISING STEP FOUR: STEWARDSHIP

With the possible exception of identification, stewardship is the most important step in the four stage fundraising process. Stewardship consists of thanking the donor and being accountable to the donor for using the donor's gift according to the donor's desire. One of the best ways to steward a donor is to help the donor to experience the positive impact his or her gift has had on the world. A common maxim is to thank the donor seven times in seven different ways. This is a good goal. Industry best practice says that a donor should be thanked within 24 hours of making his or her gift. As a general rule the sooner a donor is thanked for his or her gift the more likely he or she is to give again and to increase the value of his or her gifts. Thank as quickly as possible. Develop a formal process for thanking donors. The person who solicited the gift should thank the donor as soon as the donor says yes. Next the donor should get a phone call from an agency leader such as a board member or senior staff person saying that their gift is appreciated and will make the world better. The donor should receive a formal thank you letter that can serve as a tax receipt as quickly as possible, ideally the letter will be sent within 24 hours of the agency receiving the funds. Then the donor should be invited to participate in events such as dinners, open houses, galas, etc. The donor should be invited to view the impact his gift is having by taking a special tour of the agency or being invited to view a special video that highlights the work the donor is funding. The donor should receive mailings describing the good work that his or her gift is making possible. The fundraiser should continue to meet with the donor and show the donor the latest annual report or special article about the donor's impact and share anecdotal stories about the agency's work – telling the donor – you made this happen, thank you!

Remember that after the donor makes a major gift, every interaction that donor has with your agency is a stewardship action. If the donor calls your general information number to get some information about an upcoming

event and is treated rudely by your agency staff – that is a negative stewardship action. Or if your donor sends a letter or e-mail to your office that goes
unanswered, that is negating your positive stewardship efforts. This is why a
well-run nonprofit will treat every phone call, letter and e-mail it receives with
the utmost importance and care. Sometimes the things that cost an agency
a Major Gift are long wait times on the agency's telephone line or a delay in
processing incoming e-mail. The development department may be doing all
kinds of great stewardship work, but when the donor called the main number
he was treated rudely or had to wait 25 minutes for his call to be answered.
That one act by a temporary worker answering the phone can undo years of
major gift cultivation and stewardship.

That observation highlights the point that stewardship eventually leads
us full circle in the four stage fundraising process. Because the most likely
prospects for a major gift are people who are already good donors many of
the donors in the stewardship cycle will be identified as major gift prospects
again. The act of making a major gift will increase the donor's linkage to your
agency. The donor now feels much closer to your agency because he or she
has invested in your work with a gift of significant size. Your communication with the donor throughout the cultivation, solicitation and stewardship
process has also increased the donor's linkage. As you share stories with the
donor about the impact his gift is having you are taking action to increase his
linkage and interest. Thus, stewardship leads to cultivation and eventually
solicitation for the donor's next gift.

That said, if stewardship is done poorly, your prior major gift donors will
be the least likely candidates for new Major Gifts. If your donors gave a major
gift to your agency and then felt that they were treated poorly they are very un-
likely to give again. If your agency treated them very well during cultivation
then stopped communicating with them after solicitation they may rightly
feel as if they were just "used for their money" which is the opposite of donor-
centric fundraising. If an agency is good at getting Major Gifts from donors
but not getting those same donors to give again it is a good sign that they need
to improve their stewardship work. Sadly, this most commonly happens with
donors who are former board members. Often a new board member will be

cultivated and asked to make a major gift during his or her term of service on the board. The donor makes the gift and is highly connected to the agency during his or her board service. The board member/donor is invited to all the events, receives all of the mailings, and is the first to know about any new program. Then the donor's board term expires. His or her name is dropped from the mailing lists, he or she no longer gets invited to come to any events, no one from the agency calls or e-mails because they are busy with the new board members. The donor is left with a plaque on the wall honoring his or her board service and the feeling of being an unappreciated "has-been." This happens because the agency is viewing this person as a former board member instead of as a current major donor. Again, this agency-centric view must be replaced by a donor-centric view. When major donors end their term of board service the level of attention they receive from the agency should not decrease. Instead it should rise to a new level as the agency plans to cultivate this person for his or her next major gift. An advantage to directing Major Gifts to your endowment fund is that you can always have a stewardship visit with your donor to show them the performance of his or her endowed fund. That gift is generating earnings that are making the world better every year, so there is always something new to talk about on a stewardship visit to a major gift donor who has given to your endowment, which hopefully all of your board members do during their term of service.

Chapter 3

* * *

PLANNED GIFTS AND OTHER METHODS TO MAKE A MAJOR GIFT

MAJOR GIFT TOOLS OR HOW CAN A DONOR MAKE A MAJOR GIFT?

As noted earlier in this text, the options available to any specific donor will differ depending on the laws governing charitable giving where the donor lives as well as on the specific gift acceptance policy of your nonprofit agency. The laws of the donor's country and state determine what gifts he or she can legally make and your agency's gift acceptance policy determine what type of gifts you are willing to accept. Your agency needs to decide for itself what types of gifts it will and will not accept. These decisions must be made before you talk with donors about Major Gifts and they need to be codified in an approved policy that is uniformly followed. This practice will ensure that your fundraising efforts are as effective as possible because everyone will be "playing by the same rules." A sample Gift Acceptance Policy for small to medium sized nonprofits is found in chapter eight.

As I tell my donors, I am not an attorney. I am not an accountant nor am I a financial or tax professional. I do not give legal, tax or financial advice. In the paragraphs below I simply share what an effective Major Gifts Officer should know about the various types of Major Gift tools that are commonly used by donors to accomplish their philanthropic goals. The tools that will be described in this chapter are: 1. Major Gift Pledges 2. Gifts of Stock 3. Bequests 4. Life Income Agreements. 5. Donor Advised Funds 6. Other gifts including gifts of real estate and IRA rollover gifts.

PLEDGES

Allowing donors to make a Major Gift via a multi-year pledge is perhaps one of the most donor-centric approaches to major gift work. To simplify accounting and ensure standard practice and fair treatment of all donors each agency should define the terms of pledges it is prepared to receive. Each agency must define the smallest gift that may be paid via pledge and the maximum amount of years a pledge may last. For instance, an agency may say gifts of $25,000 or more may be paid over a period of five years or less via pledge. The agency should design a standard pledge form that can be filled out for each Major Gift pledge to state the total value of the gift and the agreed upon payment schedule. It should contain instructions on how the donor is to make each payment including the address where the donor should send his annual pledge payment and the contact information for a staff person who can answer any questions that may arise during the pledge term. The donor should then sign and keep a copy of this form for his records, and a copy should be retained by the agency in the donor's file.

Donors typically want to do pledges for two reasons. The first and most obvious reason is due to cash-flow. While most Major Gifts are made from accumulated assets, not all are made that way. Some are made from income. This could be viewed as a situation where the gift meets the definition of an agency-centric major gift but not a donor-centric major gift. Many times such gifts are made to the agency's annual fund for this reason. Other times the donor wants to accomplish a lasting philanthropic goal such as creating a named fund within the agency's endowment fund, but instead of using accumulated assets, wants to use income to do it over a period of years. The pledge allows the donor to do this, and is one reason I say that the Major Gift pledge is one of the most donor-centric tools in the Major Gift Fundraiser's tool box. Note, in the latter case, if the pledge is especially large, the agency may ask the donor to make a provision in his estate plans that if the pledge is unpaid at his death that his estate will fund the balance of the pledge at that time. This should be presented from a donor- centric approach as a step to ensure that the donor's important philanthropic goal is accomplished no matter what happens.

The second reason a donor may wish to make a Major Gift via pledge has to do with our tax code. Some very generous donors may max out their charitable tax deduction for a given year and may therefore want to spread their Major Gift over several tax years to minimize their tax burden and maximize the charitable impact their money can have in our world. Also, some donors are wise enough to realize that they want to give a certain amount to charity each year and they know that amount in itself is not enough to justify itemizing their taxes instead of just taking the standard deduction. Therefore rather than receive no tax benefit by making their charitable gifts every year they "save up their charitable giving" by making no charitable gifts for two or three years then in the third or fourth year they give all of that saved money to charity in the same tax year. This way they benefit from taking it as an itemized deduction that specific year. They then make no charitable gifts for the next year or two and repeat the process. A pledge agreement can allow a donor to make gifts on the time table that works best for her – whatever her motivation. Pledges also help the agency to know when it should expect to receive the donor's gift and that allows the agency to plan and budget accordingly. Pledges are obviously good for those reasons and they are also very good because they require good communication between the donor and the nonprofit. That communication strengthens the donor's relationship with the gift officer and build's the donor's trust in the nonprofit. This builds the donor's linkage with the agency in a very powerful way and makes the person an even better and bigger donor in the long run. For these reasons, I encourage nonprofits to make liberal use of the Major Gift pledge.

GIFTS OF STOCK

For most donors, funding their charitable gift using appreciated securities is a very smart move. I work hard to inform all of my donors about this option and encourage them to consider if this is the best option for them. I am always surprised when I mention this idea to a donor who has made many charitable gifts to various nonprofits over the years and learn that the donor had previously never knew about this option. That tells me that we, as an industry, need to do a better job of informing our donors about this giving option.

How it works. Let us say that Joe bought 1000 shares of stock at $5.00 per share and has owned that stock for several years. The stock has increased in value and now has a value of $10.00 per share. Joe is a great investor. He has doubled his money! If he were to sell that stock now he would have to pay long-term capital gains tax on the realized appreciation of the stock that he sold. Of course, he could then give that money to charity and possibly take a charitable tax deduction on his INCOME taxes for the amount of the gift but he would still have paid the capital gains tax. Paying the capital gains tax would reduce the amount of money he got from his investment and thereby lower the amount of money he could give to charity. The smaller his chari-table gift, the less his ability to impact the world according to his values (IE: the fewer hungry children he can feed).

Instead of selling the stock and giving the money from the sale to charity let us suppose that Joe gave the stock directly to a nonprofit. In that scenario Joe realized no capital gains because he never sold the stock. Therefore he owes no capital gains tax. The nonprofit will sell the stock and use the money from the sale to accomplish Joe's philanthropic goal. Because the nonprofit is tax-exempt it does not have to pay capital gains tax either. The nonprofit will provide a receipt to Joe for the value of the stock he gifted (average price the stock held on the day the nonprofit received ownership of the stock) and, assuming that Joe received no goods or services in exchange for his charitable gift, he can take the full value of the stock he gifted off his federal and pos-sibly his state income tax as a charitable deduction. Even though he only paid $5,000 for the stock he bought years ago, today Joe was able to use it to make a $10,000 gift to a nonprofit to accomplish his philanthropic goal. He was able to take an income tax deduction of $10,000 and he never had to pay a dime in capital gains tax. You can see why this option is so popular. Both outright gifts and pledges can be funded using appreciated stock.

Not all of our investments double our money. In fact, sometimes we have depreciated investments. What about those? How can a donor use depreciated stock to accomplish his or her philanthropic goal? It is rare, but occasionally I will be asked this question. As always, I encourage donors to speak to their own financial, legal and tax advisors. In this case I suggest they speak with their trusted professionals about selling the depreciated stock, deducting the loss on their income tax then giving the money they received from the sale of the stock to charity and taking the appropriate income tax deduction for that gift.

BEQUESTS

Not every major gift is a bequest but using the donor-centric definition of a major gift, every bequest is a Major Gifts because it is made from the donor's accumulated assets and not from the donor's income. Bequests are the Major Gift that almost any donor can afford to make and we sell our donor's short if we do not make sure that they know how they can accomplish their philanthropic goal with this tool. Bequests are the most common Planned Gift. Throughout my career as a Major Gift Fundraiser, I estimate that about 60% of the gifts I have raised take the form of a bequest. I mentioned earlier that when we identify a donor who has high interest in our mission and high linkage to our agency but does not have high ability that the donor is likely a good candidate for a bequest. First, let me dispel the myth that bequest prospects should be old. I will do that by sharing the stories of two different donors who I had the privilege of working with who have chosen to accomplish their philanthropic goal via bequest. Of course, donors of advanced years are good candidates for bequests also! But, since we naturally tend to think of them, I will share stories of bequest donors who do not fit the stereotype.

Jill was in her mid-40's and was identified to me as a Major Gift prospect by a team of donors I had trained to identify Major Gift prospects using the information that this book shares in section about prospect identification. The volunteer who told me about Jill said she had very high interest in our mission and very high linkage to our agency. He was unsure about her level of ability but since I had said "ability does not matter" he had identified her as a prospect for me to cultivate. I sent her a letter requesting a meeting and we met for breakfast at her favorite café one Sunday morning in the springtime. We discussed the great work that our agency does. She told me about how she got involved with our work and how much meaning the work that our organization gives to her life. It was clear my volunteer had correctly determined that she had high interest and high linkage. Then she said the magic words "I just wish I could do more!" That was when I had the opportunity to say "Well, maybe you can." Her eyes lit up. "How?" she asked. I then told her about our Endowment Fund. I explained that when gifts are made to that fund, they are never spent. Instead they are invested and the earnings from those funds are used to pay for the good work our organization does every year – into perpetuity. I explained that there are two ways to fund a gift to our Endowment Fund. "The first is simply to give money to the fund now", I said "but the second is just as powerful and that is to make a provision in your estate plans for money to come to our organization after both you and your husband have passed on. By funding the gift that way, you can be sure you have the resources you need throughout your life and afterwards you know that the good work you care about will continue on in your name." I could tell she was thinking about what I was saying. Then I said "Do you happen to have a 401K retirement plan?" She said she did. I then explained that if she made our charity a beneficiary of that retirement account then at her death one of the first things to happen would be that the administrator of her account would give that money from her 401K directly to our nonprofit. That money would then go into the Endowment Fund to accomplish her philanthropic goal. I also explained how if she took no action and let the money in her retirement account simply go into her estate, that her estate would have to pay federal income tax on all of the money in that account as it would be considered ordinary income in the year of her death. That would mean that 39.6% of that entire account would go to federal income tax. Instead, she could use the funds in that account to accomplish her philanthropic goal by simply making our charity the beneficiary of that account. To say she was delighted would be an understatement. She had always WANTED to make a major gift to our organization but did not think she could do it. She knew that our organization was making the world the way she wanted the world to be and she always wanted to do more – now she knew how she could do so! I encouraged her to talk with her own financial and tax advisors and consider making a bequest to our organization as I had described. A few days later she called me and said that she had designated a percentage of her 401K plan to come to our organization at her death. The current value of that gift was $100,000 and that number will likely to rise over time as her fund grows with the market.

The second story is about a man in his late 30s named Nick. When we met he had just had his first child and owned his own small business. He knew he needed life insurance so he bought a policy that was big enough to meet the needs of his family if anything should happen to him. When we met on a sunny summer afternoon he said that of all the things he could leave his child in the event of his untimely death, an example of how he should live was the most important. Because Nick values the charitable work our organization does he made the first $50,000 of his life insurance policy payable to our organization to establish a fund within our endowment in his name. That way if anything happened to him, then his child would receive an annual report from our agency sharing examples of the good work that "dad's fund" had done that year in his name.

Neither of these donors would have made Major Gifts of cash at that time in their life. However both were very happy to make bequests. Most importantly they accomplished their philanthropic goals in the way that was right for them at the time that was right for them. The agency I served at the time received Major Gifts that it would not otherwise have received because it engaged these rather young bequest prospects. Long ball is the name of the game in Major Gift fundraising, especially in the realm of Planned Giving.

Another point however is that now that these donors are on that agency's list of bequest donors they will get extra attention from the agency in the form of stewardship mailings and gift officer visits. This will build their linkage and interest. At some point as Jill and Nick get older and more established in their careers it will be easy for a gift officer to then talk to them about funding their bequest in cash during their lifetimes. By securing a bequest gift from a young donor today we make it easier to secure a cash gift from them in the future. Remember – be donor-centric. Help the donor make the gift that is right for him or her today.

There is an argument that bequests from younger donors are not valuable because the donor likely has many years to change his mind and remove your charity from his estate plans. To that I say two things. First, none of us know when we will die and it is foolish to think that everyone will live to be 90 years old. In fact, I recall a situation where I worked with a donor in his early 50s to do a $25,000 bequest to my organization's endowment fund and he died of a sudden and unexpected heart attack only a few months later. My stewardship visits were with widow to whom I shared a copy of his named fund's performance report and talked about the good work that Jack's fund was able to do that year because Jack was generous and thought ahead. Second, if your agency plans on doing such a poor job of stewarding your bequest donors that they want to cut you out of their estate plans then shame on you! I generally find that my bequest donors choose to *increase* the amount of their bequest to us each time they modify their estate plans because their linkage and interest in our work has grown thanks to our stewardship efforts. In fact, working with donors to increase the size of their existing bequests is a very frequent part of a Major Gift Officer's work.

You will notice that in the examples above neither Jill nor Nick needed to modify their will or living trust. For the majority of donors a bequest in the form of a beneficiary designation makes good sense and can be done quickly and easily. I remember one donor visit I had when iPads were first becoming popular. I was meeting with the donor over breakfast at a small diner in Northern Virginia on a winter morning. While I was talking with him about our Endowment Fund he took out his iPad and started tapping on it. At first I was a bit annoyed as I thought the behavior was rude. But, being the good Gift Officer, I ignored the tapping and pretended not to notice that he was staring at his screen instead of looking at me. After a few minutes he said "Ok. That's done" and turned the iPad around so I could see the screen. While we were talking he had logged on to Vanguard.com and made my organization the beneficiary of his IRA. It was really that simple. These days I am hopeful and not annoyed when a donor takes out an iPad mid conversation.

Of course for some donors the best way to make a bequest to charity is using their will or living trust. I always like to be sure donors know that my organization is happy to recognize either a first or second to die bequest. This means that the donor can choose when my charity receives their gift. They can design their estate plans so that all or part of the gift comes to our organization when they die or not until both they and their spouse have passed on. This flexibility is appreciated by donors whose primary concern is to ensure that their surviving spouse has the assets he or she needs. It also results in larger gifts because once the donor knows he does not have to worry about providing for his spouse he is free to dedicate more of his estate to our charity. Some donors will establish a trust in their estate plans that is designed to pay income to their children as long as their children are alive and then make a payment to our nonprofit only upon the death of their children. This allows the donor to take care of their children and still accomplish their philanthropic goal. I also encourage donors to make a bequest of a percentage of their estate, policy or account instead of simply giving a fixed amount. The benefits of that method are many. First, it allows the size of the gift to keep pace with the times. Let's say the donor cares very much about your agency so he makes a bequest of $75,000. That may be 20% of his estate today. If he simply made a bequest of $75,000 and his estate grew over time the percentage of the estate that is going to accomplish the donor's philanthropic goal naturally decreases. If the donor's estate doubled in size, the gift that was valued at 20% of the estate when the will was drafted would now only be a tenth of the estate. Have your donor's philanthropic feelings fallen by 50% ? Of course not! Many donors will want to use a percentage bequest so that their values are reflected in their estate plans no matter what the size of their estate may be. As the value of their estate rises (or falls) the amount of their charitable bequest will rise and fall, always reflecting the portion of their estate they wish to use to accomplish a charitable goal. This is a very donor-centric approach to requesting bequest amounts and in most cases a percentage bequest will ultimately result in more money going to do good work in the world than a simple bequest of a specified cash amount would. When donors make a bequest using the percentage method, I ask them what the estimated current value of that gift would be today for the purposes of our records and for donor recognition. If they tell me it is $10,000 today I thank them and make sure they know that the next level of recognition in our nonprofit's multi-tiered bequest recognition program is $25,000. I ask them to please inform me when their bequest value reaches $25,000 so that we can honor them with membership in the next level of our bequest recognition program. As donor's assets appreciate as the markets grow they call me and we update our records, celebrate their new level of bequest giving recognition and enjoy a great opportunity for further stewardship and often cultivation. It keeps the relationship between donor and gift officer active.

It is a good practice to provide donors with sample language that will help them add your charity to their estate plans. Information such as the legal name of your organization, your address and federal employer identification number are helpful to donors. I encourage donors to keep the language in their estate planning document very general. I ask them to use language that simply gives our organization the gift they want our organization to receive. I then work with our donor to draft a second document that directs our organization to use the gift according to the donor's specific wishes. The donor retains a copy of that document in his or her records and a copy is kept on file at our office. When the gift is received that document will direct how our organization is to use the bequest (IE: create a fund bearing the donor's name within our Endowment Fund or to support a specific area of our work). Every organization I have worked with has allowed its donors to get more specific with their dedication requests as the amount of their gift increased. This practice ensures that the nonprofit does not bear too heavy of an administrative burden trying to administer particular small gifts. It also ensures that the agency have enough money in an endowed fund to accomplish a specific goal. For instance, if a donor wants to fund a certain scholarship each year, the size of that fund needs to be at a minimum value or it will not generate enough earnings to accomplish the donor's goal. Good nonprofits will not allow a donor to restrict a gift that is too small to have impact. Instead they will pool smaller gifts together so the donor can have the impact he or she wants to have while still making the gift that is the right size for him or her. This practice incentivizes giving at higher levels and most importantly helps the agency to have lasting positive charitable impact in our world.

LIFE INCOME AGREEMENTS

Life income agreements come in two main forms, namely; charitable gift annuities (CGAs) and trusts. We will discuss CGAs first.

LIFE INCOME AGREEMENTS - THE CHARITABLE GIFT ANNUITY

Every nonprofit will determine its own age and minimum gift size requirements for charitable gift annuities. Each nonprofit will also set its own payment rate based on the donor's age. It is considered best practice to follow the guidelines established by the American Council on Gift Annuities on such matters. Many nonprofits require Charitable Gift Annuity donors to be at least 55 years of age to do a Charitable Gift Annuity and require the minimum gift size to be $10,000. It is also common to allow donors to do either a single or two life annuity contract. In the case of a two life CGA the payment rate may be lower than it would be on a one life annuity but the donor has the peace of mind knowing that as long as either he or his spouse/partner survive they will have annual income from the nonprofit organization. At present a 50 year old donor could expect to find an annual payment rate of 3.7% and a 90 year old may expect a rate of 8% with a Charitable Gift Annuity. These annuity rates are offered in June 2015, a time when Bank of America's current 9 month CD rate is only 0.04%.

A donor making a major gift using a Charitable Gift Annuity will make a gift to your nonprofit. In exchange for that gift your nonprofit organization will enter into a contract with the donor whereby the donor becomes the annuitant. Your organization agrees to pay the donor a certain amount of money each year in exchange for the donor's initial gift to your organization. This annuity contract is legally binding. Your nonprofit organization is legally obligated to make the annuity payments regardless of how the market is performing or what your financial condition is. For that reason only large, stable and mature nonprofits are able to offer the option of Charitable Gift Annuities to their donors. Some people like to explain the concept of a CGA by using the illustration of an apple tree. They say the donor gives the apple tree to the charity and in return the charity gives the donor a specific number of apples each year as long as the donor is alive. Life income agreements in general and charitable gift annuities in particular are good gifts for donors who need the income from their assets but who do not actually need to own the asset itself.

An additional benefit of charitable gift annuities is that donors may take a tax deduction for a portion of their gift and a portion of their annual payments will not be subject to federal income tax.

Let us assume a donor who is 50 years old wants to make a $50,000 gift using a charitable gift annuity. He gives $50,000 to the nonprofit organization today. He is entitled to take a tax deduction of $9,758 on his federal income tax this year (up to 50% of his adjusted gross income of course). Additionally, he will receive a payment rate of 3.7 percent. That means that every year that the donor is alive the nonprofit organization will send him a check for $1,850.00. Of that amount, $1,219.15 will not be subject to federal income tax until the donor reaches his predicted life expectancy.

Some donors ask why they cannot deduct the entire amount of their gift when doing a Charitable Gift Annuity. The answer is because the donor will be getting something from the nonprofit in return for his gift. I like to use the example of Girl Scout cookies because buying a box of Girl Scout cookies is an experience common to almost all Americans. I say that if you buy a $10.00 box of cookies you may only deduct $5.00 from your taxes because you ate $5.00 worth of cookies. This example usually helps donors understand why only a portion of the gift they gave to establish a CGA is tax deductible. Their disappointment at this fact is usually overcome when they learn that a significant portion of their annual payments will not be subject to federal income tax.

Donors who are good candidates for Charitable Gift Annuities are people who have charitable intent (high linkage and high interest) and who also have the need for guaranteed income. Many donors have money sitting in banks earning very low rates of return at the moment. When they learn they can accomplish their philanthropic goal AND earn relatively high rates of guaranteed return – they are overjoyed.

I have worked for membership based organizations where members pay annual dues. I have had several donors figure out the size of the gift they needed to make to do a CGA that would pay them the amount of their annual dues each year. They like making a charitable gift and then getting a check each year that they can use to pay their dues. They feel this is a very efficient choice because it accomplishes their charitable goal and as they say "I was going to pay my dues anyway!"

It should be noted that in the example above the donor funded his Charitable Gift Annuity with cash. The donor can also fund his or her CGA with appreciated stock. While the donor will not totally avoid capital gains tax as if the donor made the gift outright, the donor will be able to spread the capital gains tax out over time by funding a CGA with appreciated assets.

LIFE INCOME AGREEMENTS – THE CHARITABLE REMAINDER TRUST

While only donors to large and established nonprofits can use Charitable Gift Annuities to accomplish a philanthropic goal, donors to any nonprofit in the United States can use a Charitable Remainder Trust. Again, I feel I must emphasize that I am neither an attorney nor an accountant. The following description of Charitable Remainder Trusts is designed to be a VERY SIMPLE overview of a gift tool that many donors may find helpful. The good Gift Officer needs to know the basics about such instruments so that the Gift Officer can encourage the donor to speak with his or her own financial, legal and tax expert to see if using a tool like this would work well for them.

CRTs can be funded with many different kinds of assets including cash, stock or even real estate. When the donor gives to the Charitable Trust he may be eligible for a tax deduction. If the trust is a Charitable Remainder

Unitrust (commonly called a CRUT) the donor will receive an annual income based on a percentage of the trust's value. For instance a donor may establish a CRUT to pay him 5% of the trust's value each year. No matter what the value of the trust is that year, the donor will be paid 5% of that value. Or the donor may choose to use a Charitable Remainder Annuity Trust instead. The CRAT will pay a fixed amount of money to the donor every year no matter what the value of the trust is. CRUTs offer the potential for larger payments when the value of the CRUT is high because the market is healthy. However donors with CRUTS may be disappointed with the size of their annual payments during years of poor market performance. Of course, what assets are in the trust and how those assets are invested will greatly impact the rate of growth. CRATs give the security of fixed payments but run the risk of being depleted by poor market performance combined with a high annual payment rate. Many donors will choose to use a CGA instead of a CRAT because the CGA offers fixed payment rates without the same risk as a CRAT because the CGA payments are backed up by the full faith and credit of the nonprofit organization that has contracted with the donor whereas the CRAT is only worth the assets in the trust. With either the CRUT or the CRAT, as with the CGA, the non-charitable beneficiary (usually, but not always, the donor) receives income while they are alive (for the donor(s)'s entire life or for a period of time defined in the trust documents) and when the trust expires (usually at the donor's death) the money that *remains* in the trust goes to the charity. That is why these gift types are called Charitable *Remainder* Trusts. Donors who give using CRTs have similar traits as donors who give using CGAs. The main difference being that it generally takes more money to fund a CRT than it does a CGA because the gifts made to the trust are kept in the trust and the earnings from the gift are used to make the annual payments to the donor. Therefore CRT gifts tend to be much larger than CGA gifts. Also, donors who believe in the power of the market to grow wealth will likely choose to use a CRUT because their gift can grow as the market grows and the amount of money they receive each year will correspondingly grow, since they will always receive a percentage of the trust's value. Donors who like a lot of security will prefer the CGA where their annual payments are backed up by the full faith and credit of your nonprofit and they will stay away from the CRUT with its potential for lost value. It is important to know that there are usually four parties involved with a gift using a trust. The first is the donor. The second is the income beneficiary (usually but not always the donor). This is the person(s) who receives the money that the trust pays out each year. The third is the nonprofit who will receive the money left in the trust when the term of the trust expires (usually at the donor's death). The fourth is the Trustee who administers the trust. Sometimes the Trustee is the nonprofit who will receive the money, but other times it is a different party.

A donor couple I will call Ted and Linda had a unique circumstance. They both shared a philanthropic passion that aligned with the work of the nonprofit I worked for at the time. Because of that they had always been good donors. Now they were at a stage in life where they wanted to accomplish a philanthropic goal and ensure that Linda had additional income in her later years if Ted (who was considerably older than Linda) should predecease her. They accomplished that goal with a Charitable Remainder Trust. Their trust will continue to give an annual payout to Linda as long as she is alive then the money that remains in the trust will be used to accomplish the philanthropic goals that Ted and Linda held dear.

LIFE INCOME AGREEMENTS - THE CHARITABLE LEAD TRUST

When I started working in this sector, the federal estate tax exemption was only $650,000. I was, at the time, working for a nonprofit whose donor base was largely comprised of mid-western farmers. Almost all of them had estates worth more than $650,000 because the farm land that they depended on for their living was so valuable. Back in those days it was not uncommon for a donor to make a gift using the Charitable Lead Trust. In that case the donor would make a charitable gift (possibly land) to his charitable trust. The asset would stay in the trust for a period of years. While the asset was in the trust it would generate money that was given to the donor's chosen nonprofit. When the trust term expired, the asset passed out of the trust to the non-charitable beneficiary, usually the donor's children or grandchildren. Because the payments made from the trust go to charity and the assets remaining after the trust expires will go to a non-charitable party, this type of trust is called a charitable LEAD trust. Giving in this way had tax advantages that allowed the donor to minimize or avoid federal estate tax liability. Like CRT's, CLT's involve four parties. They are the donor, the charity receiving income from the trust, the trustee who administers the trust and the non-charitable party who will receive the assets from the trust when the trust expires. Today the federal estate tax ceiling is high enough that 99.5% of all estates will not owe any federal estate/gift tax so we see fewer donors using this tool to accomplish their philanthropic goals than we did 20 years ago. My personal favorite experience with a CLT involved a farming family in Indiana. The oldest generation of the family who owned the land are the people I will refer to as the donors. They were ready to retire. Their sons did not want to farm as they had careers of their own. However their grandchildren were still in school and the donors did not want to sell the farmland because there was a chance that their grandchildren would want to carry on the family tradition of farming. The family was also very dedicated to the nonprofit I was serving at that time and wanted to contribute strongly to our capital campaign. This was also when the estate tax exemption was much lower than it is today. The solution was found in the form of a Charitable Lead Trust. The family gifted the farmland to the CLT. The trust rented out the farmland and directed the income from the land to our capital campaign. When the trust expired the land would pass to the donor's grandchildren having avoided the estate/gift tax. This allowed that family to contribute significantly to our capital campaign and keep their farm in the family for the next generation. While the tool is not that common anymore, I still work with some donors for whom this tool makes sense, so it is good for the Gift Officer to be aware of its use.

GIFTS OF LIFE INSURANCE

There are two ways a donor can use his or her life insurance policy to accomplish his or her philanthropic goal. The simplest way is for the donor to simply make his or her favorite nonprofit a beneficiary of all or part of the insurance policy. This can be done with any type of insurance policy and is a great way for many donors to achieve their philanthropic goals. This type of giving vehicle is especially appealing to two types of donors. The first group of donors who find this giving method appealing are donors like Jeff. Jeff owns his own business and is the type of employer who cares deeply about his employees. He realized that because his business is a professional service firm that if he died his employees would be out of work. He decided to take out a sizable life insurance policy so that if anything did happen to him the policy could be used to pay each of his employees a severance check to ensure they are financially sound while they hunt for new jobs. That policy is quite large and in addition to using it to take care of his employee's needs, Jeff decided to use $250,000 of that policy to accomplish a long held charitable goal. Jeff is very concerned about a country in Latin America because of a personal connection he has to that land. He dedicated $250,000 of his life insurance policy to go to a nonprofit that works in that country. As Jeff said, "While I'm alive, I travel and take mission trips each year. This bequest ensures that work can continue after I'm gone."

The second group of donors for whom insurance makes a good gift vehicle are donors like Stan. Stan bought a life insurance policy years ago when his children were young and his house was mortgaged. He wanted to make sure that if, God forbid, anything should happen to him that his family would be okay financially. He bought the policy and thankfully never needed it. Today his children are grown and his house is paid for. Today that life insurance policy that his family no longer needs can be used to accomplish his philanthropic goal by making his favorite nonprofit the policy's beneficiary.

Donors like Stan may even want to give ownership of their policy to your nonprofit in addition to beneficiary designation. It is important to note that this is not an option for term life insurance as that type of life insurance has no actual cash value. To better understand how this works, let us think about life insurance for a moment and realize that there are three parties in a life insurance contract. The **owner** of a life insurance policy is the one who has the rights that are stipulated in the contract. These include the right to name a beneficiary; the right to participating dividends; the right to surrender the policy for its cash value; and the right to transfer ownership. The **insured**, who is often the owner of the policy, is the person whose death causes the insurer to pay the death claim to the **beneficiary**. The beneficiary can be a person, trust, estate, business or nonprofit organization. If a donor wishes to give ownership of the policy to the nonprofit and the nonprofit is willing to accept the gift, then the donor may take a tax deduction for the value of the gift. In some cases, the donor may gift a policy that is not yet fully paid and then continue to pay the premiums and deduct the cost of paying those premiums from his taxes because he is paying the premiums on a policy that is owned by the nonprofit. Many nonprofits only agree to accept life insurance that is not fully paid if the donor agrees to make a gift of at least the cost of the annual premium to the nonprofit each year or agrees to continue to pay the premiums until the policy is fully paid for. Several years ago many nonprofits accepted ownership of life insurance policies only to find out that the administrative burden of owning the policies out-weighed the value of accepting the gift of ownership. Today most nonprofits will only accept ownership of life insurance for donors who are of advanced age. For other donors, it makes more sense for the donor to keep ownership of the policy and simply make the charity the beneficiary. This is a topic that each nonprofit must explore for itself and address in its gift acceptance policy. Life insurance is a gift type that many donors do not think about. A donor-centric Major Gifts effort helps donors use the asset that is right for them to accomplish their philanthropic goal. For many donors that asset is life insurance.

IRA ROLLOVER GIFTS

In some years, The Congress of The United States passes a bill that the president signs into law allowing the charitable IRA rollover, or qualified charitable distribution (QCD). These laws allow certain donors to exclude from taxable income – and count toward their required minimum distribution – certain transfers of Individual Retirement Account (IRA) assets that are made directly to public charities. This is a great way for just about any donor over age 70 ½ who has to take a required minimum distribution from his or her

IRA to make a charitable gift. In years past the maximum amount that could be given was $100,000 and the gift could not be used to fund a life income agreement. Because this way of giving is not permanently codified, donors can only take advantage of this way to give in the years when congress and the president both act to make this possible. The donor whose story I shared in the opening sentences of this book used this vehicle to make his $100,000 major gift to honor his late wife. Personally, as a Gift Officer, I keep a list of every major gift donor I have discussed this option with throughout the year. I also watch the news like a hawk and as soon as I see that congress and the president have acted to allow donors to give this way, I immediately contact each person on that list and let them know. This usually results in at least one or two major gifts each year that giving this way is allowable. Groups such as the Partnership for Philanthropic Planning are actively engaging with congress to make this type of giving a permanent part of our tax code. As of July 2015 they have yet to succeed.

DONOR ADVISED FUNDS

Donor Advised Funds, frequently called DAFs are great alternatives for donors who would like to have some of the benefits of having their own foundation but do not want or cannot handle the administrative burden of maintaining a foundation. I have heard DAFs described as "Charitable Checking Accounts" because they are simply holding pens for charitable dollars. DAFs are helpful for donors who need to make a charitable gift in a certain year for tax reasons but do not want the charity to actually receive the money until a later year. Perhaps they do not know which charity they will give that money to and so they put it in their DAF and take their time deciding which charity should receive it. The donor can give money to the DAF in the year he wants to take the tax deduction. The money can stay in the DAF earning interest until the donor directs the DAF to make a grant to the nonprofit. Many large non-profits and community foundations offer Donor Advised Funds as services to their donors. Many for-profit financial institutions also offer DAFs to their customers. If a donor has a DAF that tells the gift officer that the donor is a

Major Gift prospect because clearly the donor has the ability to make a major gift or he could not have funded a DAF (most DAF's require an initial gift of at least $10,000 to open the account). The donor has charitable intent or he or she would not have opened the DAF. The fact that a donor has a DAF also tells the Gift officer that the donor thinks seriously about his charitable giving. Finally, having a DAF means that the donor has money ready to give to charity sitting in an account that he has earmarked for that purpose. Ability is established for DAF holders, next the gift officer must determine if that donor has linkage to that gift officer's nonprofit and interest in the mission of that gift officer's nonprofit. Two important things for every Gift Officer to know about Donor Advised Funds are that DAFs can only make grants to US charities and donors cannot pay legally binding pledges to a nonprofit from a DAF.

GIFTS OF REAL ESTATE

Earlier we addressed the benefits of donating appreciated securities to a nonprofit to accomplish a philanthropic goal. Another appreciated asset that few donors initially consider when deciding how to fund their major gift is what may be their most appreciated asset, their real estate. Under specific circumstances a gift of real estate can be a very good way for a donor to make a Major Gift. At the most basic level, it makes sense to gift real estate when the property in question has significant long-term appreciation, such that the owner would incur a sizable capital gains tax upon selling it, and when the property is relatively easy for the charitable organization to liquidate, with minimal chance for incurring liability or major carrying costs prior to the sale. Your nonprofit's Gift Acceptance Policy needs to govern the ways that donors can use their real estate to accomplish their philanthropic goals through your organization. Obviously, larger better equipped nonprofits are generally better prepared to handle a gift of real estate. However even small nonprofits can do so and sometimes such a gift can be transformational for them and the people they serve.

Chapter 4

● ● ●

CAMPAIGNS

There are two basic schools of thought surrounding campaign goal setting currently in vogue. The first school of thought is the "shoot for the moon and you will hit the stars" model. The second model is the "set yourself up for success model." We will now explore each of these models and then discuss a different approach that I believe is more effective than either one.

Proponents of the Shoot for the Moon model will say that by setting a "stretch goal" they will challenge the donors, volunteers and staff to work as hard as possible and raise as much money as possible for the campaign. People of this mindset will frequently say that the large size of the goal will inspire people to go the extra mile. These goal setters will often privately tell their staff and donors "it is a stretch goal. We will be happy with whatever comes in. We just want to do our best." While some people may indeed be motivated by being part of a campaign with a large target goal, this method is fret with potential problems. If this method is taken in determining a campaign goal, extra effort must be taken to ensure that the common pitfalls of this method are avoided. We will now consider some of those pitfalls.

A very common problem for nonprofits that use "shoot for the moon" fundraising goals relates to their budgeting process. Sometimes the people who set the campaign goals are not the same people who make the agency's budget. Often times, the people who are budgeting income will look at the public campaign goal and set that number as their projected income goal. They will then build a budget around that "stretch" number and when the goal is not met the agency is in a world of hurt because they had budgeted to spend the money that was never raised. This puts the agency in crisis and in extreme cases can cause an agency to collapse. Sadly, I have seen this happen enough that I know this is not a rare occurrence. Other times, the agency will not use the public fundraising goal number in their budgeting but will rather build a budget based on historic income projections instead of campaign goals. This conservative approach has the advantage of avoiding the pitfall described above however it has its own potential problems. An astute donor or board member may compare the budget to the fundraising goals and find the incongruity upsetting. Such a person may ask why an agency is saying one number publically but then using another (smaller number) privately. They may ask "where is all that extra money going?" I have seen this situation happen and it can lead to distrust between donors, staff, board members and the agency's community. At the very least the disconnect this method creates between fundraising and budgeting can be confusing. Consider explaining to a donor that you are doing a $5 Million campaign this year, then showing that same donor your audited financial statements and budget as part of your annual report, and the donor seeing that you only plan to spend $1 Million that year. The donor would wonder "where is the rest of the money going?" A good fund raiser could certainly explain the difference between the goal and the reality, but that is a conversation I would rather not have to use my limited donor cultivation time to address. It has the potential to derail a gift conversation and can be avoided if the agency plans better.

Directly related to the problems described above is the danger of "integrity fatigue" that comes from announcing unrealistic numbers as part of a public campaign. This is much like the boy who cried wolf. If donors know your agency frequently announces large goal numbers and then fails to meet them your donors will become fatigued with hearing about large numbers from your agency. They may even start to distrust your public information. The donor may think "Every year they say they are going to raise $2 Million and they never do. Now they are saying they fed 1000 homeless people last year. Did they really do that or is that another made up number like their fundraising goal? Are their service stats inflated by 50% like their fundraising goals are?" Please understand my point; I am not saying that it is unethical for a nonprofit to use public "shoot for the moon" style campaign goals. I am merely saying that doing so does present problems and can be confusing to donors. In the most extreme case, a donor may view such a method as misleading and therefore consider it to be unethical because they have been confused by the contradiction between your public campaign numbers and the smaller numbers in your audit and budget. That is the last thing any nonprofit wants. Knowing this, it is a good practice for nonprofits to plan around these pitfalls when organizing a campaign.

Of all the downsides to the "shoot for the moon" goal setting method the one that is the worst is that when the large goal is not met the donors, volunteers and staff who participated in the campaign feel as if they have failed. Since how donors feel is very important to successful fundraising the effects of this impact can be catastrophic to a nonprofit's donor base. Consider the graphic below. It is based on an actual sign I saw in a small mid-western town for their community fund campaign several years ago. The sign said "0 days left in campaign. 70% of goal reached. Thanks for trying!"

How do you think the donors who made Major Gifts using their hard earned accumulated assets felt when they saw that sign? I doubt many of them felt good about their philanthropic choice. I bet many of them felt like a failure instead of a generous success who took positive action to make their community a better place. People who set stretch goals with the idea that they will still feel successful if they don't meet the goal need to realize that most donors do not share that way of looking at things. Most donors do not have the benefit of knowing that even meeting only 70% of the goal represented the best fundraising year that agency ever had and that its programmatic impact will now be stronger than it ever was in the past because of the money raised in that campaign. All the donors who saw that sign knew was that they only got to 70% of the goal. In school that would be a grade of C minus, just barely passing. Some donors will simply stop giving because they are discouraged. Sometimes donors who gave more than others to the campaign (which they now view as a failure) will start to feel resentful towards the donors who gave smaller gifts or to the campaign's potential donors who did not choose to give. They will feel that way because the large gift donors will feel that the donors who did not give as much caused the campaign (and by extension the donor who made a major gift to the campaign) to fail. I have seen this happen. I have also seen this anger directed towards the nonprofit's staff. I have heard board members say things like "Since Joe has been the Executive Director we have never met a fundraising goal" when considering the Executive Director's request for a raise. Of course the nonprofit had also raised more money than it ever had before under this Executive Director's leadership but because of their "shoot for the moon" goal setting method board members felt like the executive director had failed in fundraising because goals went unmet. While there may be cases when a stretch goal is appropriate, it is my opinion that in most cases the negatives outweigh the positives and that a "shoot for the moon" goal setting approach should usually be avoided.

The other method currently in common usage when setting campaign or fundraising goals is the method I refer to as the "set us up for success" method. This method is, in my opinion, a far superior method than the "shoot for the moon" method. We will now discuss the "set us up for success" method and then discuss the third method that I believe is the most effective way to set campaign and fundraising goals.

The "set up for success" method is, in some ways, the opposite of the "shoot for the moon" method. In the "set up for success" method the goal is set so low that the agency is always sure to exceed it. Because this is basically the opposite of the "shoot for the moon" method all of the downsides of the "shoot for the moon" method described above, are basically positive advantages of the "set up for success method." If an agency takes the campaign goal and uses it to budget income in their annual they will find themselves with a budget surplus. Donors are not confused by seeing a big number in the fundraising campaign literature and then seeing smaller numbers in the agency's financial reports leaving them to wonder "where the other money went." If a board reviews an executive director on his or her ability to meet fundraising goals the employee will score well. Most importantly; donors, volunteers and staff who participate in this campaign will feel successful and not feel like failures. In fundraising, like most of life, success begets success. Therefore an attitude of excitement, optimism and possibility are fostered in the donor base and development staff.

Every coin has two sides and this method of goal setting is no exception. Sometimes the "set us up for success" goal model can result in there being no real "GOAL" just a number that is called goal that everyone knows will be exceeded. Many people call this style of goal setting "lazy" because they say it requires no work, just let nature run its course and voilà a goal is met. This can be a danger. In some instances using this goal setting method can result in a campaign failing to reach its full potential because people stop giving and/or working towards the campaign goal after the finish line is crossed. While it is the better of the two methods, it is not without its flaws.

One flaw common to both the "shoot for the moon" and the "Set up for success" methods is that the goal generated from either method is not very helpful for agency budget setting. The "shoot for the moon" goal is obviously dangerous as it can lead a nonprofit to expect more money than it is likely to receive. The "set up for success" model is also poor for this purpose because it will underestimate the agency's likely real income. Because the definition of a budget is a plan for income and spending if the agency budgets for less money than it will actually receive it cannot plan as effectively to use that money to accomplish its philanthropic mission as it could if it had a fully accurate picture of its annual income from fundraising. In short, the more an agency knows about its income, the better it can plan to use it, the more effectively it can accomplish its philanthropic mission the better tool it is for a donor to use to accomplish his or her philanthropic goal. Donor-centric nonprofits have accurate and healthy budgets. Therefore, it is ideal when a fundraising goal can help our agency develop its budget.

The method for campaign goal setting that I suggest is not an easy one. I call it the "trinity method" because it requires the agency to develop three separate dollar figures based on data analysis. It requires an agency to collect and analyze data as well as plan its work in great detail. It also requires the agency to follow the plan it develops. Not every agency is capable of doing this. If an agency does not have historic giving data it cannot use this method. In that case I suggest the agency use the "set up for success" method of setting an obviously obtainable goal until it has collected enough giving data to move on to the more complex "trinity" method. Some agencies have the data they need to follow this method but are unwilling to do the extra work it requires or are unwilling to commit to following a plan instead of simply shooting from the hip as they are used to doing. I believe the extra work required for this method is worth doing.

The method I suggest will involve three separate numbers. That is why I call it the "trinity method." Through data analysis and planning you will arrive at three different numbers for your campaign. The highest number is for internal use only and is called the "Internal Maximum Goal." The middle number is called the "Stretch Goal." The lowest number is your conservative minimum fundraising projection. The lowest number is also your "Public Goal."

The highest number is only used internally and represents the most amount of money you could possibly expect to raise in your campaign. This number will be close to the "shoot for the moon" number with the difference being that through data analysis you have been able to show that it is possible to reach this target. This number is called the "Internal Maximum Goal." I suggest using this name because it communicates that this number is only for agency internal communication and should not be shared publically. This figure represents the best your fundraising department could ever do if everything went according to Hoyle based on data analysis. In other words, every donor will always say yes and give the amount you ask for when you ask for it. Because we live in the real world, we do not really expect to reach this potential, just as we do not expect every school student to have a 4.0 GPA even though it is theoretically possible for every student to have one. Development Staff will see this number, as will Finance staff and the Executive Director. Board members may see it in private briefing documents. The general public and your donor base will not see this number.

The second number is your "Stretch Goal." This number goes on the thermometer on the courthouse lawn above the 100% mark. If you reach this figure, your campaign thermometer will be full of red at the 125% mark, over flowing with abundance out of the top of the gage. If your donors meet the stretch goal your agency will be able to perform "extra services" which you then describe in detail. This number is used in budgeting, but is not the exclusive number used in budgeting.

The third number is your "conservative fundraising projection" and is your "Public Goal." This number is 100% of the goal on your thermometer sign and is close to the "set up for success goal." This number is one you expect to slightly exceed based on analysis of your data. When this number is reached your campaign will celebrate success and at the same time announce that you are very close to achieving your stretch goal. You will explain that by meeting your public goal your donors have successfully ensured another year of operation for your agency, or the accomplishment of your campaign's main priorities. Now you are entering the stretch phase of the campaign where special projects can be funded. This figure is used in budgeting as well. As you have probably figured out, your budget will plan to fund "special projects" with the money raised during the stretch phase of the campaign.

Let us now explore how each number is derived. The first step in developing a fundraising campaign is called "qualifying your prospects." For an annual appeal it may be as simple counting up everyone in your database who will receive your appeal letter. In a major gift campaign it involves making a list of people you will cultivate and solicit for a major gift as part of the campaign. In a complex campaign it will be both annual fund, major and planned gift prospects all separately qualified and considered with a specific individual donor-centric plan made for each planned and major gift prospect. After the lists are created a projected ask amount will be assigned to each donor. These numbers are initial estimates and are subject to change. That said, they should be as accurate as possible. The total value of all of the planned asks are then totaled. This total represents your "Internal Maximum Goal" number. If you asked every person on your RADAR and every one of them said yes, this is what you would raise. This number will be very high. It is internal only so that it avoids the pitfalls described in the "Shoot for the moon" goal section of this book. It is important to establish this number because, as proponents of the "shoot for the moon" system explain, seeing the possibility of a large number will inspire people by showing a glimpse of the possible. Because you did not just make this number up, you know it is POSSIBLE although not likely that this number will be reached. It is important to know this number so that your success rate (aka hit rate) can be measured. For instance if it was possible for you to raise $1 Million and you raised $500,000 you would know that you had a "hit rate" of 50% because you raised half of the money that you could have. If next year you had the possibility of raising $1.25 Million and you raised $625,000 you will see that your hit rate was again 50%. If the third year your "Internal Maximum Goal" was $1.5 Million and you raised $750,000 you will see that your hit rate is again 50%. Next year when you calculate that your "Internal Maximum Goal" is $2 Million you can with a good deal of certainty predict that you can honestly expect to raise $1 Million based on your historic hit rate. I have just explained how you find your "stretch goal number." Your "Stretch Goal" is your agency's historic hit rate multiplied by your "Internal Maximum Goal." For instance, if your hit rate is 50% and your "Internal Maximum Goal" is $500,000 then your "Stretch Goal" would be $250,000.

Many agencies do not keep track of their historic hit rate. They cannot use this system yet. Their next step needs to be a campaign using the "set up for success" goal setting method and they need to collect data so that they can analyze it to know their hit rate for at least three years before moving to the trinity goal setting method. It is important to calculate the hit rate for annual fund, major and planned gifts separately if the campaign involves all three gift types. This is because we expect to have a higher hit rate with major and planned gifts than we do with annual fund mail appeals. I used to advise agencies to simply use the industry standard numbers for hit rate averages to calculate their predicted results for goal setting. However, over the years I have found that these numbers fluctuate too much from agency to agency and location to location for that method to be a solid one. It is best not to use this system of goal setting until an agency has at least three years' worth of its own data to analyze to determine its specific hit rate. I suggest using a five year hit rate average when possible but a three year average is acceptable. An agency should monitor trends in its hit rate for annual fund, major and planned gifts and when change is noticed investigate to find the reason for the change and do all it can to make sure its hit rate is healthy. An agency should always compare its statistics on donor acquisition, hit rate, donor retention and upgrade rate to national averages but should always remember that because all circumstances are unique the best method for predicting future performance for any specific nonprofit is to accurately record past performance and analyze those numbers to predict future trends. This is one reason a good database system is so vital to the success of a nonprofit's fundraising efforts. Data analysis is a key component of setting good goals and thereby reaching the agency's maximum potential and ensuring optimum donor satisfaction.

The "stretch goal" figure gets used in your agency's budgeting process. However it is not the base line used in budgeting. All essential line items are paid for using the lower "public goal" number. Items that are "nice but not essential" are funded by the difference between your "public goal" and this number. For instance, let us say you have computed your "Internal Maximum Goal" and multiplied it by your hit rate to find that your "stretch goal" is $625,000. Now you want to determine your "Public Goal" by subtracting

25% from your "Stretch Goal." This gives you a conservative buffer. Therefore you subtract $125,000 and define your "Public Goal" as $500,000. You design your agency's budget to pay for all of its essential items with the first $500,000 raised in the campaign. You use the next $125,000 to fund things in your budget such as a staff retreat, or extra services, or new carpeting in your offices, in other words, things that you would like to have, but can cut out if needed and still survive. This is what I call having a modular budget. Essential items in your budget should be funded by your most solid funding source. Less important items should be funded by less dependable funding sources. It should be clear which items are funded by which income items. That way if a certain income expectation is not met, it is easy to cut an expense of corresponding value and thus keep the agency's budget balanced while not cutting into vital agency functions. It is also important to fund appealing programmatic expenses with money from the stretch goal so that you can honestly communicate to your donors during the "stretch phase" of the campaign that their additional gifts at that time will have meaningful programmatic impact.

For most nonprofits the "Public Goal" should be 25% lower than the "stretch goal" By setting this lower number as your public goal you reap the benefits of the "set up for success" method but you also avoid the downsides of that method that are often attributed to a lazy development effort that fails to move donors forward in their giving by ending the campaign before it really reaches its maximum potential because you have designed a challenging "Stretch phase" into your campaign when you use the Trinity Method of campaign goal calculation. If your local economy has taken a nose dive lately you may wish to set the public goal even lower than 25% below your "stretch goal" because the hit rate percentage you used to calculate your "stretch goal" was based on asks that took place in a better economic environment. Conversely, if your economy has taken off in the past 12 months, you may wish to decrease the difference between your public and stretch goals. As a natural fiscal conservative, I am slow to suggest decreasing the difference between the stretch goal and the public goal. I believe having a financially sustainable nonprofit is one of the most donor-centric acts that nonprofit professionals can achieve. In most cases 25% is a good buffer and a good place to start.

To recap, your campaign planning process will start by defining the timeline and criteria for the campaign. You will decide if your campaign will have annual fund, Major Gift and/or planned gift components. You will then qualify your prospects in each category based on their linkage, interest and ability. For the annual fund component this may simply consist of looking at your data base and finding how many donors you are going to send mailings to. You then look at your historic hit rate for that type of ask. Let's say you are going to mail 15,000 letters to existing donors asking each donor for a gift of $75.00. To calculate the "Internal Maximum Goal" number for the Annual Fund part of your campaign you should calculate how much money you would raise if every person you asked said yes and gave you the amount you asked for. In this example, if that happened you would raise $1,125,000. That number is your "Internal Maximum Goal" for the Annual Fund part of your campaign. Next, you know that your agency's historic 5 year mail appeal hit rate for existing donors is 30% and that your average mail appeal gift size is $50. You calculate the "stretch goal" number for the annual fund section of your campaign by multiplying the letters you are sending by your hit rate. So we multiply 15,000 letters times a hit rate of 30% and get 4500. You predict that 4500 people will say yes to your request for a gift in the Annual Fund Mailing. You know your average mail appeal gift is $50.00 so $50.00 times 4500 = $225,000. This number is your "stretch goal" number for the annual fund part of your campaign. You want to give your agency a 25% buffer between your "stretch goal" and your "public goal" so you subtract $56,250 from the "stretch goal" to get $168,750 as our annual fund "public goal" part of the campaign.

The next part of your campaign is the Major Gifts section. Unlike in the Annual Fund section of the campaign where you look at large numbers and calculate percentages based on aggregate data, in the Major/Planned gift sections of the campaign each major donor will be considered individually. Let's suppose you have 10 major gift prospects for this campaign. Based on your understanding of their linkage to your agency, interest in your agency's mission and their ability you have decided that each of these donors will be solicited for a major gift during the campaign. Again, the donor's readiness for solicitation determines if they should be in the campaign or not. You do not ask a donor for a gift because it is campaign time. Instead you include a donor in the campaign because he or she is now ready to be asked during the period of the campaign and has philanthropic goals that align with the charitable work the campaign will fund. It is donor-centric. For illustration purposes, let us assume that you have ten major donors in this campaign. 5 of them will be asked for gifts of $25,000 each. 3 will be asked for gifts of $10,000 each and 2 will be asked for gifts of $100,000 each. That makes your total major gift ask amount $355,000. Therefore $355,000 is the Major Gift part of your "Internal Maximum Goal" number. You know from data analysis that your agency's three year major gift solicitation average hit rate is 70%. You multiply $355,000 by 70% to get your Major Gift portion of the "Stretch Goal." In this case that number would be $248,500. You want to make your "Public Goal" 25% lower than that number so the Major Gift section of your "Public Goal" would be $186,375.

If your campaign included planned gifts, you would do the same thing for planned gifts. Since this is a simple illustration we will omit that work in this text and assume that there is no Planned Gift component to this campaign. Let us now combine all of the numbers we reached through data analysis and form our campaign goal using the "trinity" method.

Annual Fund Internal Maximum Goal: $1,125,000.00
Major Gifts Internal Maximum Goal: $355,000.00
TOTAL INTERNAL MAXIMUM GOAL: $1,480,000.00

Annual Fund Stretch Goal: $225,000.00
Major Gifts Stretch Goal: $248,500.00
TOTAL STRETCH GOAL: $473,500.00

Annual Fund Public Goal: $168,750.00
Major Gifts Public Goal: $186,375.00
TOTAL PUBLIC GOAL: $355,125.00

The "Public Goal" is used to fund your nonprofit's basic activities or the campaign's core objectives if this is not campaign to fund an annual budget. When the "Public Goal" is met the campaign celebrates success and enters the stretch phase to fund other important priorities that you will share with your donors in detail. The money that is raised during this part of the campaign is directly tied to specific budget items so that they can be funded if the money is raised and will not be funded if the money is not raised. At least some of these items must be items that will inspire donors to share generously. Your "Stretch Goal" is calculated by multiplying your historic hit rate by your "Maximum Internal Goal." Your "Internal Maximum Goal" is calculated by counting up the amount of money you would raise if every person you ask as part of the campaign said yes. In addition to being used to calculate your hit rate, it is used to inspire your nonprofit's leadership by showing them what the true possibilities are.

As you can see by keeping good records and analyzing them to form campaign goals we are able to accurately predict future success and notice any trends that might need our attention before they become obvious problems (such as a decrease in hit rate, a decrease in the number of annual fund or major gift prospects). We are also able to communicate goals that are based in reality and still challenge us to reach our full reasonable potential for each campaign. We do our best to ensure that all involved in the campaign feel good about their giving and their participation.

Chapter 5

EVENTS

In some parts of the United States special events such as galas or grand balls comprise a very large part of many nonprofit's fundraising efforts. This is truly lamentable as such affairs are rarely donor-centric at all. Let us consider the typical gala fundraiser. The nonprofit secures a desired venue, usually at considerable financial cost, and always by consuming many, many staff hours. After that the nonprofit sells tickets to the event. It may give its highest donors free tickets. Then the nonprofit hires a graphic designer to create a program book for the purpose of selling advertising space in that program book to gala sponsors. The nonprofit's staff and volunteers then spend many, many more hours asking local businesses to buy an ad space in the program book by assuring them that there will be an audience full of potential customers to read their advertisement. To make sure that those customers do indeed want to buy tickets and come to the event, the nonprofit needs to make sure that the food, drink and entertainment for the event are amazing. More money and time are spent on catering, bartending and event planning. Sometimes volunteers and staff use their time and money to secure silent auction items as well. Then the day of the gala finally comes. Guests attend (having paid for their ticket), eat some shrimp and drink some Riesling. They think the jazz band sounds nice and they visit with some friends from work who also bought tickets. Maybe they bid on a silent auction item then they go home. Your nonprofit pays all of its bills, finds it has some money left over – declares the fundraiser a success and starts planning for next year. If you have done these sort of events in the past, you know that my assessment is accurate – and that there is nothing donor centric about this form of "fundraising" at all.

The fundraising gala is not donor-centric because nothing about the gala really connects your donors to your mission and nothing about the gala facilitates your donors accomplishing their philanthropic goals. Oh, you might have a speech or show a video highlighting your agency's work, but for all the money and time you spent to make the gala happen, that is hardly enough donor-centric activity. Your staff and volunteers spend hundreds maybe even thousands of hours working on a gala and at best such an event gives your attendees 20 minutes of exposure to your agency's mission. Nope, even highlighting your nonprofit's work at your gala cannot make it a donor centric fundraising activity in my mind. Of course you want your gala guests to give you money – you even ask for it! However, you are not asking them to invest in the future of the world by making a philanthropic gift to your nonprofit because your nonprofit is doing effective work to make the world align with your donor's core values. Instead you are asking your donor to buy a ticket to your event because you will have great desserts, a full bar and a live band. You tell your "corporate sponsors" that you have a product they want to buy – namely the audience who will read your program book. You are no different than the newspaper who will also sell them ad space. Many people who are fans of gala type fundraising remind me of how much money is raised and therefore used to do good in the world with galas each year. To them I reply, if the same amount of money and energy had instead been invested in a truly donor-centric fundraising plan, over the long run, more donors would be engaged with a donor-centric message and the nonprofit would grow a healthy base of donors who choose to make annual fund, major and planned gifts to that nonprofit in order to accomplish their philanthropic goals. Nonprofits who rely totally on the gala method of fundraising may find that they really have no individual donor base at all. Instead they have two customer bases, one who likes to eat shrimp cocktail and another who likes to sell ads to people who eat shrimp cocktail. A nonprofit in that condition, needs to start from ground zero and build a donor centric Annual Fund system that will eventually grow Major and Planned Gifts.

There are three types of events that I find appropriate and helpful in a donor-centric fundraising plan. The first is the Annual Dinner. The second is the Million Dollar Dinner and the third is the Fireside Chat. We will now explore each of these donor-centric events in some detail.

The Annual Dinner differs from the gala because its primary focus is to say "Thank you" to the people who have made charitable gifts and volunteered with your nonprofit over the past year. Typically the dinner is not overly fancy and "thank you" awards are given to the nonprofit's donors and volunteers. The Annual Dinner usually costs the nonprofit money as the invitees are provided with complementary tickets to the dinner as a "thank you" for their support. This is a cost of doing good stewardship. This event builds interest and linkage for the people at the event because it provides a time for your existing donors to be with other people who also share their philanthropic priorities who also know your nonprofit. Existing donors may invite perspective donors to attend the event as their guests. You steward your donors by saying thank you in a way that many find meaningful. You connect your donors with the volunteers and staff who perform the actual work of your nonprofit. Meeting these people increase your donor's linkage. The Annual Dinner usually features a speaker who praises the work that the agency has done and reminds all present that the work was made possible by donors. This inspires donors to share even more generously. Some agencies find the cost of the Annual Dinner prohibitive. While I consider it a very good use of your development office's stewardship budget, I have seen the cost of the Annual Dinner successfully off set with a mail appeal directed to a subset of donors (such as board alumni). The mail appeal highlights the value that volunteers and supporters provide through their hard work throughout the year. The ask of the appeal usually says something like "Say thank you to the volunteers and supporters who accomplish our mission every day with your gift of $35 to pay for a volunteer's dinner."

The second event that can play a very important role in a donor-centric fundraising plan is the "Million Dollar Dinner." There are many ways to successfully conduct a Million Dollar Dinner and many books have been written on the topic. The following is a basic plan that usually works well. Most Million Dollar Dinners count the value of bequests as well as cash gifts. In fact, if your nonprofit is trying to start its endowment fund, the Million Dollar Dinner may be a great tool for you to use. The Million Dollar Dinner is led by a committee of ten people. Each of those people is a "table captain." They each must commit to an outright gift or a bequest of $10,000 or more to your nonprofit's work. Each of them will host a table of ten. That means each table captain needs to identify, cultivate and solicit a gift of cash or a bequest of $10,000 or more from 9 other people. That makes 100 donors each giving at least $10,000 to raise the $1 Million. Most Million Dollar Dinners take about one year of regular work to accomplish. At the conclusion of the campaign the donors gather for a nice dinner together to celebrate the fact that collectively they raised $1 Million and hear a speaker who will celebrate the work that the nonprofit does in the world and how that nonprofit is now even stronger thanks to the generosity of the donors at that dinner. Usually donors ultimately cover their own meal costs. The organizing nonprofit chooses the venue and pays for everything up front then the donors who took part in the campaign who wish to actually attend the dinner simply reimburses the nonprofit for the meal cost. The section of this book that deals with Identification, Qualification, Cultivation, Solicitation and Stewardship can be helpful to teams wishing to conduct a Million Dollar Dinner. The event is very donor-centric because the major and planned gifts that are being celebrated at the dinner were raised in a donor-centric fashion. The donors gathered at dinner are doing so to celebrate that they have taken a step to accomplish their philanthropic goal.

The third event that I have found very helpful in every nonprofit fundraising position I have ever held is an event that goes by many names. Some people call it a "fireside chat" others a "soiree" others a "house party." The event can actually take many forms, but it always involves a small to medium size group of major/planned gift prospects meeting at the invitation of a person they know and respect for the purpose of learning more about the nonprofit's work. For the purpose of this writing, I will simply use the term "fireside chat" to refer to this type of event. I generally find a donor who will host the fireside chat in his or her home on a Sunday evening, around 7:00 PM. Sunday evenings are usually good because most families do not plan activities at that time and it is after the dinner hour so most people will not arrive at the event expecting a full meal. That time and day are not locked in stone, but just a general rule. I provide the host with a list of potential invitees. I put the names of donors on the list who live near the host who have a long history of good giving to the Annual Fund but have not yet recorded a bequest or Major Gift with our nonprofit. I may include the names of people who have recorded a relatively low value bequest. I also add the names of some strong Major Donors who can be in the room as an example of a person who has accomplished a philanthropic goal through our nonprofit already. I then provide that list to the host without telling the host why each individual was put on the list. I then inform the host that because it is their event, in their home, they may certainly add and subtract from that list as they like. I merely offer it to them in an attempt to be helpful. The host then sends invitations to the people he or she chooses and records their RSVP's. Most hosts I work with choose to use e-mail to invite their guests, but some do use paper invitations as well. Still others simply phone everyone on the list and invite them. I find it is most effective when the host extends the invitations and truly serves as host for the event. People are more likely to enjoy an event that their friend hosts than they are to enjoy an event that is simply held at their friend's house. The host then tells me how many people will be there and, when possible, gives me names so I can ensure that all of the guests are entered into our database so that our interactions at the fireside chat can be accurately recorded. Most hosts chose to provide wine and cheese type of refreshments to their guests. Some will opt for coffee and cake instead. Those choices are always left to the host. I bring a copy of our most recent literature designed to inform potential donors about the impact our nonprofit is having in the world. The first 30 minutes of the evening are generally spent in informal conversation and socializing. I like attendance at these events to be between 6 and 20 people. It takes me about 30 minutes to "work the room" having a brief conversation with all in attendance and exchanging business cards. Once that happens, the host will call the meeting to order by thanking the guests for their attendance and introducing any dignitaries that may be in attendance such as a director from our agency's board. Then the host introduces me and I thank the host and invite all of the guests to give the host a round of applause for hosting such a lovely event so generously. I then introduce myself and thank the people present for their history of support to our nonprofit. I then introduce our Endowment Fund to them. Most of the donors in the room have only made gifts to the Annual Fund and are unaware of the options they have for long-term philanthropic impact using our endowment. I explain how a gift to our Endowment Fund made from accumulated assets during the donor's lifetime or via bequest can accomplish the donor's philanthropic goals in very powerful way. I share examples of other donors who have made that choice. I invite donors who are present who have made that choice to share a few words about why they chose to give in that way. I then conclude by sharing a story of our nonprofit's impact. I speak for about fifteen minutes, including a time for Q&A at the end of my planned remarks. Then I inform everyone that there is literature for them, including my business card (although I tried very hard during the first 30 minutes to give each person there my card when we were introduced) by the food table. I encourage everyone to enjoy the rest of their evening visiting, and to let me know if they have any questions as I will be available for one-on-one conversations for the rest of the night. Then the event goes back to socializing. It usually lasts another 30 minutes. Usually, I spend the rest of the night talking with people who approach me. When everyone has left, I ask the host for a full list of names for those who attended. I then send each person a thank you card the next day, with my business card again. I usually get several calls or e-mails over the next several weeks from people who attended the event who want to talk about making a Major Gift or bequest. I thank the host, sometimes sending a vase of flowers to the host the next day as a thank you for his or her generosity.

Fireside chats do not have to take place around a fireplace. In fact, attending a "fireside chat" in Charleston, South Carolina in August may not sound that appealing to donors. At least not as appealing as it may sound the donors in Minneapolis in January. Find a name that works well for your event. I have done coffee and donuts in the morning with some groups and cocktails and appetizers in the evening with others. I have had events in bank lobbies after hours, in nonprofit facilities on the weekend, in donor's offices during the workday and in donor's homes in the evenings. While each event is unique, I generally find that events in the evening in a donor's home tend to work best.

Chapter 6

● ● ●

METRICS

We get the behavior we incentive and one of the biggest ways to incentivize a specific behavior is to measure that behavior and hold ourselves accountable to meet certain measurable goals. As a society we are moving into an age of "big data" and the value of good data that can be accurately analyzed to inform decisions is becoming better understood each day. A donor-centric fundraising program needs to develop donor-centric metrics and design a system to accurately record those metrics. The leadership of that nonprofit must frequently study their nonprofit's results in order to understand the health of their fundraising program and make changes when needed so that their agency is able to accomplish the philanthropic goals of its donors in the best ways possible. Good metrics are like gages on a car, they can show a problem before it becomes serious thus allowing an adjustment to be made before there is a catastrophic failure. Metrics in the donor-centric fundraising office have the added value of being able to quantify the work that gift officers are performing. Many people, including board members and nonprofit CEO's do not understand how fundraising works. They do not understand how development directors spend their time and seeing these metrics can help them understand the work that the development staff performs and how the development office forms the engine of the nonprofit's income by helping donors achieve their philanthropic goals. Measuring a development officer's performance based on their donor-centric actions incentivizes that development officer to behave in a donor-centric way. Tension frequently arises in nonprofits where development officers want to treat their donors in a donor-centric way but are required to achieve certain bench-marks that are not donor-centric. In order to achieve those benchmarks development officers have to treat their donors in ways that are not based on the donor's desire to share a philanthropic gift but instead are based upon an agency's time-line. This is not a good practice as it stops the nonprofit from fulfilling its ultimate purpose which is to be a tool for donors to use to improve their world according to their values. For instance, if a nonprofit tells its gift officer that he must ask for a $50,000 gift each month the gift officer will do that, even if that means asking a person for a $50,000 gift who should have been asked for a three year pledge totaling $100,000 but payable in gifts of only $33,334 per year. Because the agency would not consider that pledge part of the gift officer's benchmark goal because that year's income to the agency would be a gift under $50,000, the gift officer may be pressured to ask that donor for a one time gift of $50,000 instead of the three year pledge that is in the donor's best interest. With that example you can see how non-donor-centric benchmarks incentive behavior we do not want and fail to serve our donors (or our nonprofits) well in the long run. Many nonprofit board members and executives say that they agree with that statement in concept, but they need some concrete way to measure a gift officer's success rate. They are absolutely right. A donor-centric fundraising department is not a department void of benchmarks and goals. It is a department with bench-marks and goals that are donor-centric and incentivize behavior that focuses on meeting the long-term philanthropic goals of the nonprofit's donors. In this chapter we will explore in detail what items a donor-centric nonprofit should measure, how it should set goals and measure performance.

The reports offered in this chapter as examples in this chapter the current year's performance as compared to the performance of past years so that trends can be identified and considered. These reports are donor-centric because they focus on the behavior of the nonprofit's donors not the internal goals of the agency and they measure the interactions that agency staff have had with donors that is designed to help donors accomplish their personal philanthropic goals. To illustrate how a report can be either donor-centric or agency-centric let us consider the following two examples. Example one is a very common agency-centric report that a board may review. "Our agency has raised $25,000 which takes us to 40% of our Direct Mail goal this year and puts us 10% ahead of where we were last year." Notice how the entire focus of that sentence is on the agency and its need to receive. Instead a donor-centric report would say "Our donors have given $25,000 through this year's mail appeal which is an increase of 10% over what our donors gave last year. That means our donors have already accomplished 40% of the annual goal for giving via Direct Mail." Both of those statements communicate the same facts. The first example presents the facts from an agency-centric viewpoint and the latter example from a donor-centric view.

Below is a spreadsheet full of statistics that a well-run nonprofit should collect, track and use to measure and plan its fundraising work. By studying the spreadsheets in this section the reader can learn the specific data points that his or her nonprofit will need to collect to generate this report. If the reader's nonprofit does not currently collect the data needed to generate reports like the ones below, the reader will need to start doing so. It is important to collect this data and store it in such a way that it can be easily accessed for study and analysis as shown below. To do this, the nonprofit will need to use a good database system. A good exercise is to take the spreadsheet charts in this chapter and try to fill them out for your agency's most recently completed fiscal year. If you find that you cannot answer a question because you lack data, you are not alone. Many nonprofits I have worked with over the years find that they cannot complete these reports because they have not tracked the data they need to analyze to complete these reports. If that is the case, find out what specific data you are missing and design a new plan to collect and store that data for future years. Make your goal to be able to complete the reports in this chapter easily at any time. I suggest that these numbers should be reviewed weekly by the

Development Director and monthly by the Executive Director and Board of Directors. When I served as a Development Director I prepared documents just like the ones in this chapter for our Executive Director and our Board every month. The sample below is what an end-of-year report should look like, you can easily envision how this report could be formatted to become a monthly and year-to-date report for any nonprofit you work with. The information in these reports can be used to predict future performance for your fundraising efforts, changes in trends can show the impact that changes in your nonprofit's behavior is having on your donors. Did you increase the frequency of your newsletter mailing last June? If so, have you noticed a corresponding increase in your donor retention rate? The numbers in this report can also be used to measure your agency's actual progress against the budgeted projections that were used to create your agency's annual budget. You will note that I do not expect the board members and volunteer leaders of the nonprofit to automatically know if the numbers they are viewing are good or not. That is why I suggest putting a paragraph under each set of numbers briefly telling the board member reading the report what he or she was looking at. This is important because many board members (like people in general) will not ask a question in a group setting if they think they are the only person who does not understand the report they are viewing. This can result in an entire room of people looking at a report they do not understand, none of them asking for clarification because each person assumes that he or she is the only person who does not understand the report. This can lead to boards making bad decisions because they do not understand the information they need to understand to inform a good decision. This failure to understand reports can lead to bad situations where board members blame staff saying "you never told us this information!" and staff blaming board members saying "we sent you the reports every month for three years! How did you not know we were having problems?" That is why when giving reports to others, especially board members or volunteers, it is important for nonprofit staff to make it easy for them to understand the data being reported by being as clear as possible in the text of the document as illustrated below.

FUNDRAISING ANALYTICS 2008 – 2010 REPORT PRESENTED IN JANUARY 2011
DONATIONS FROM INDIVIDUALS

Year	Total Number of Donors
2008	1547
2009	1542
2010	2396

Comments: This statistic shows the total number of giving units who made a gift in the stated calendar year. It is composed of repeat and new donors. This reflects both donor loyalty and new donor acquisition. The higher this number is – the better.

Year	Donors Lapsed (1 year inactive)
2008	603
2009	568
2010	583

Comments: This shows the number of donors who had given in the prior year but did not give in the current year. It includes donors who made only one gift, and those who had a history of giving but did not give in that calendar year. The lower this number is - the better.

Year	Donors Reactivated
2008	196
2009	250
2010	341

Comments: This shows the number of donors who had given at some point in time (from 2004 on) who did not give in the prior year, but did give in the current year. The higher this number is - the better.

Year	Donors Upgrading
2008	334
2009	237
2010	1160

Comments: This shows the number of donors who gave more in current year than they had in prior year. The higher this number is, the better.

Year	First Time Donors
2008	226
2009	249
2010	687

Comments: This shows how many people made a gift for the first time in the current year. The higher this number is the better.

Year	Avg. Donation Size
2008	222.80
2009	193.97
2010	116.04

Comments: This shows the average amount that a donor to our nonprofit gives per year. Our Avg. Donation size has gone down because of the high number of new donors. New donors give at lower levels than established donors and form the base of our development pyramid. This is not a bad thing – as long as donor upgrade rates are rising (they are), and new donor acquisition rates are rising (they are) as reflected in the total number of donor's rising as it is.

Because "Automatic Giving" programs (where donors signed up to give a small gift from their credit card automatically every month) are the future of the Annual Fund and a very large part of the Annual Fund today, I suggest collecting and reporting the following data on your agency's Automatic-giving program. Below is a chart showing the metrics that a well-run nonprofit would want to view about its automatic-giving program in January 2011. A side note, the nonprofit would not call its program "automatic-giving." Instead it would have a simple and appealing name for its program that reflects the values and culture of its program. The National Public Radio station in Chicago calls its automatic-giving program "High Fidelity." I know of a religious nonprofit that calls its program the "Forever Faithful." I use the generic phrase "automatic-giving" in this text rather than the name that any specific nonprofit might use to describe their recurring giving program for the sake of simplicity and so that we all know what we are talking about in this text.

Metric	Value
Number of Automatic-givers in January 2009	146
Number of Automatic-givers Lost to death in 2009	4
Number of Automatic-givers who quit giving by choice in 2009	9
Number of New Automatic-givers in 2009	39
Number of Automatic-givers in January 2010	163
Number of Automatic-givers who upgraded at end of 2009	3
Number of Automatic-givers in January 2010	163

Amount Received through Automatic-giving 2008	$58,447.00
Amount Received through Automatic-giving 2009	$57,494.00
Amount Received through Automatic-giving 2010	$68,387.00
FUTURE PROJECTION FOR 2011 (January's actual income * 12)	$71,635.00

As mentioned in the section of this book that addressed the Annual Fund, paper mail appeals are still at the heart of most Annual Fund systems in 2015 and will remain so for many years. The following chart shows metrics that a well-run nonprofit would present to its Board of Directors each month. The chart below represents the important metrics to measure and monitor for any mail appeal campaign.

MAIL APPEAL ANALYTICS FOR "END OF YEAR MAILING"

Metric	2008	2009	2010
Gross Income	35,896	28,225	48,801
Cost	3,580	3,525	3,781
Letters Sent	6,977	5,406	8,793
Net Income	32,316	25,772	45,020
Number of Gifts	346	299	461
Avg. Gift Size	104	94	98
Cost Per Dollar Raised	0.10	0.12	0.08
Cost Per Letter	0.51	0.47	0.43
Return on Investment	903%	731%	1190%

COMMENTS TO ACCOMPANY THE CHART OF STATISTICS:

Mail Appeal EOY: This mail appeal may be our biggest fund development success of the year based on percentage increase over prior year. This happened because we had built the donor base earlier in the year through Mail Appeal 3 which re-activated lapsed donors and made new donors out of long time members who had never given a gift by asking them for a $10.00 gift. The nature of this appeal (and the automatic-giver appeal) was more aggressive than we have traditionally used. The good returns for these appeals would show that this approach was successful. Note – the 2008 statistics are a bit skewed because one donor made a VERY large gift in this appeal. Our efficiency is also improving – while you can see that it is costing us less to raise money – you cannot see that it is also costing us less staff time. In 2008 the staff printed and mailed all letters in house – this took all staff many hours. Now we just e-mail the file to the vendor who prints and ships all of our materials and wait for the returns to arrive. This time saving (while at the same time saving money and producing a higher quality mailing) is invaluable.

While the metrics above are important to measure the overall health and effectiveness of your nonprofit's fundraising efforts and the success of your "auto-giving" and mail appeal Annual Fund results, it is important to also measure the work that you are doing to identify, cultivate, solicit and steward major and planned gifts. Of course while the good work you do for Major and Planned Gifts will eventually be reflected in your agency's over all metrics it is still important to measure specific actions each month.

There is an old cliché that the best time to work in a development office is 20 years after a good planned giving officer had been there. There is truth to that statement because Major and Planned gift work progresses at the pace that is right for the donor and sometimes that means the work we do today will not result in our agency seeing money for many years. Remember, our goal is to help donors accomplish their philanthropic goals not to simply make numbers show up on the balance sheet of a nonprofit corporation during a specific quarter. So, how do we measure and evaluate the work we do for major and planned gifts in a donor-centric development office?

If you are a fan of baseball you will know that the sport is a game of statistics. Several years ago Oakland A's General manager Billy Beane discovered that by analyzing certain statistics for each baseball player he could accurately predict how they would perform in the long run as baseball players on his team. Using that method in 2002 the Athletics became the first team in the 100 plus years of American League baseball to win 20 consecutive games. Since then other baseball teams have started using analytics to help their teams succeed as well. Your development office needs to measure major gift performance with a similar philosophy. Instead of just waiting to see when the run comes in, or being amazed by the occasional homerun, you need to pay attention to some metrics that may otherwise go un-noticed, metrics that when taken together as a whole, over time, indicate the impact of your major and planned giving efforts.

Major and Planned Gift work requires having a personal relationship with your donor. How else could you learn about that donor's philanthropic goals? In order for personal relationships to develop and grow, the people in the relationship must interact with each other. The gift officer therefore needs to record their personal interactions with each donor. The interaction can be either an in person meeting, a telephone call, a letter or an e-mail. Each time the gift officer uses any of those methods to communicate with a donor it should be recorded.

Every time a Major Gifts Officer has a professional interaction with a donor the action should be classified as either a; Cultivation, Solicitation or Stewardship action. Because the longest parts of the donor cycle are Cultivation and Stewardship, most of the gift officer's actions should be in those two categories. Personally, as a full time Major Gifts officer only around 3% of my actions are solicitations. That is not because I have few solicitations! It is because I have MANY cultivation and stewardship actions.

By tracking the actions described above, you can generate a report each month that shows the following information.

Interaction Type	Cultivation	Solicitation	Stewardship
In person meeting	8	3	9
Telephone conversation	15	0	35
Letter	45	0	10
e-mail	150	0	200
TOTAL	218	3	254

You can see that this gift officer had a total of 475 donor interactions last month. 45% of her actions were Cultivation Actions. 0.63% of her actions were Solicitation Actions and 53% of her actions were Stewardship Actions. If I was her supervisor I would be happy with these numbers. Further analysis shows that she does most (if not all) of her solicitations in face-to-face meetings. Because common knowledge within the industry shows that face-to-face meetings are most effective for major gift solicitations I am happy to see that. Assuming that an average month has 22 work days in it, this gift officer averages just fewer than 12 donor interactions per day. If she works a 7.5 hour work day that averages to 1.5 donor interactions per hour. Considering she has to enter her actions into the database, plan her work, strategically think about what she is doing and ensure her work is at the quality that the donor deserves, I'd say she is working close to full capacity. 73% of her donor interactions happen via e-mail. That is why she is always on the computer! She is not playing Solitaire or on Facebook after all! If I were her supervisor I would want to ask her about her donor e-mails because this percentage is rather high. She would likely tell me that she sends lots of internet links, videos and articles to her donors that show the donor examples of work the agency is doing that the donor cares about. Many of those donors reply to her e-mail and she then briefly communicates with them via e-mail to schedule an in person meeting for a future time.

If you have multiple gift officers at your agency you can compare their actions to one another and see if a particularly successful gift officer has some numbers that stand out from the rest. Be warned, that every gift officer's donors are unique and the balance of their portfolio is therefore unique. Therefore, not every gift officer's action record should be identical. For instance if Gift Officer A has older donors than gift officer B, it is reasonable that Gift Officer A would send more paper letters and fewer e-mails than his colleague whose donors are younger and therefore more likely to be tech savvy. Major Gift work is always about the needs of the donors.

The next metric to measure is called "hit rate." It is simply the percentage of solicitations where the donor says "yes." Generally this is measured monthly but only a gift officer's annual hit rate is used to measure his or her total effectiveness because any given month may be unusually high or low. Generally if a gift has not been funded within 12 months of the ask it should be considered a "no." A healthy "hit rate" is generally between 60% and 80%. If a Gift Officer's annual hit rate was lower than 60% I would want to see that officer focus on performing more cultivation actions. If I was his supervisor I might give him a benchmark goal of increasing his cultivation actions by a certain number in his next review period and see if the increase in cultivation actions resulted in an increased hit rate. In most cases it will. If a Gift Officer's rate was above 80% I would measure the amount of time that his or her donors spend in the cultivation cycle. I suspect that number may be very high. In that case I would calculate the number of cultivation actions that gift officer averages prior to asking for a gift and encourage him to consider soliciting after a fewer number of cultivation meetings. In this case I would only suggest this idea to the Gift Officer for consideration; I would not require it of him. To do those things the agency need to collect and analyze data about donor-centric actions.

The chart above shows that "Gift Officer Aaron" has 2800 perspective major donors in his prevue. These may be all people who currently give $1,000 or more per year to the annual fund, or have come on his RADAR by personal referral from a board member, donor or volunteer. This is basically his "big pond picture." Of those 2800, he has identified 350 of them by analyzing their Linkage, Interest and Ability as described earlier in this book and how he has cultivation plan for each donor designed to help the donors accomplish their philanthropic goal by making a major gift or bequest. Of course, in order to do that the Gift Officer has to have personal interactions with his donors. Each of those actions is either a Cultivation, Solicitation or Stewardship action. The chart above shows how many of those donors' most recent interaction with the Gift Officer was a Cultivation, Solicitation or Stewardship action. In this case you can see that the gift officer above currently has 52% of his donors in the Cultivation Stage because the last action he had with 53% of his donors was a Cultivation action, 3% of his donors in the Solicitation Stage and 44% of his donors in the Stewardship Stage. Those are very healthy ratios, maybe even ideal ratios. This report shows that donors are moving through the cycle in this Gift Officer's care. If the Gift Officer's hit rate was above 80%, I would want to be sure that he did not have an unusually large number of people in the Cultivation Stage. A high hit rate combined with many donors in the Cultivation Stage can mean that the gift officer is not asking soon enough. As stated above, I would suggest that the gift officer in this situation consider asking sooner because as we discussed in an earlier portion of this book, it is important that the Gift Officer actually ask for a specific gift so that the donor can make an informed choice about all of his or her giving options. Sadly, I have seen too many cases where a donor makes a large cash gift only to learn after the gift is made that if he had made the gift using appreciated stock he would have avoided capital gains tax, or if he had made the gift with a different designation to the nonprofit a goal he cared about could have been accomplished better than it will be with the designation he chose when he wrote the check.

The primary job of the Gift Officer is helping donors achieve their philanthropic goals. To do that job well a Gift Officer needs to use the tools he has as effectively as possible. Tracking and measuring the metrics above will help a gift officer be more effective with his donors and can help an agency get a better picture of the work that its development office is doing. Being able to show board members metrics such as these, combined with good explanations often results in a board choosing to invest more money in fund development, thus allowing the agency to even better serve its donors (and increase the number of its donors). Therefore, it behooves every Gift Officer to track the metrics above and use the analysis of those metrics to empower them to do an even better job of helping their donors accomplish their philanthropic goals.

Today's database systems are able to provide the reports shown above without much effort, as long as every donor interaction is entered into the database properly. The days of needing to know a computer programming language or how to write complex formulas using Boolean operators to see needed data are a thing of the past. Gift Officers should be responsible for entering their actions into the database, managers or administrative staff should then be able to get all of the information described in this section by simply running a report at any time. If your nonprofit's database system does not allow for that level of functionality, I seriously suggest looking into a new system. Today's database systems cost less than ever and offer more functionality than ever before. I personally know of several database systems that could do what I just described that any nonprofit can buy today (June 2015) for under $5,000. Even the smallest nonprofit can have a donor-centric database today!

Chapter 7

❦ ❦ ❦

THE ANNUAL FUND

The Annual Fund is the heart and soul of any healthy nonprofit's fundraising effort. When the Annual Fund is healthy and is being used to fund the basic operations of the nonprofit, then the Major Gift effort is free to be totally donor-centric and make asks based on the timing preference and philanthropic goals of the Major Donors. This is of course our goal as donor-centric fundraisers and will result in more and larger charitable gifts. Unless the Annual Fund is healthy, no other parts of the nonprofit's fundraising system can be healthy.

The mantra of the Annual Fund is "Get the Gift, Repeat the Gift, Upgrade the Gift." As donors follow that process through the Annual Fund system over the course of time Major Gifts rise out of a healthy Annual Fund. If the Annual Fund is healthy your agency will have major gift prospects. If your Annual Fund is not healthy it likely will not have true major gift prospects (donors who will make gifts to your nonprofit from their accumulated wealth instead of just from their income). The Annual Fund should provide funding for the base operations of your nonprofit. The reason for that is because the income your nonprofit receives from its annual fund donors is the most dependable and it is unrestricted. It is the most dependable because it is the most diversified. Your Annual Fund donor base is very large and therefore the most diverse of your funding bases. Because it is the largest and most diverse it is the most stable and therefore should be called upon to provide the funding for your baseline, most important, essential operations. Donors to the Annual Fund understand that their gifts (which are relatively small) are combined with the gifts of others to keep your nonprofit active in doing the charitable work that the donor cares about.

The Annual Fund runs on an annual cycle timed to the financial needs of the nonprofit. That is why it is called the "Annual Fund." Let me speak about the name "Annual Fund" for a few moments. There is currently a movement in the nonprofit community to change the name of this fund to something else. Proponents of that idea say that "donor's do not give to the ANNUAL FUND, they give to the needs of the world therefore you should call your Annual Fund something like the 'Needs of the world Fund'." While that certainly sounds like a donor-centric idea, I do not think it matters what you call your agency's Annual Fund because a good fundraiser never simply asks a donor to give to a fund regardless of its name. A donor centric fundraiser always approaches the situation by asking a donor to accomplish a philanthropic goal. The word "Annual Fund" has always been an internal term to refer to a specific part of the agency's fundraising system. It is a universally accepted term that allows us to communicate across the industry using a common language. It was never designed to be a gift motivator. Asking a donor to give to the "Annual Fund" is like asking a donor to give to budget account number AB1145. It is silly, confusing and not donor-centric at all. We may invite donors to make a gift that will change the world by giving to our agency's Annual Fund, but we never simply ask a donor to give to the "Annual Fund." In that case the focus is on changing the world, not the name of the fund the donor will use as her tool to accomplish that goal. This is because we do not fundraise because nonprofits need to receive instead we fundraise because donors want to share. Nonprofit organizations are merely a conduit for the donor to use his or her money to accomplish a philanthropic goal that that he or she has. If the donor wants children in his town to have a good education he gives his money to accomplish that goal. Because he knows your school is providing a good education to the children of his town, he writes the check to your school's Annual Fund campaign. We don't ask that donor to give to the "Annual Fund" instead we ask that donor to help educate the children of his town then we tell him that he can do that by making a gift to your charity. The current movement to rename the Annual Fund has the unintended consequence that many agencies think they are now being donor-centric because they call their "Annual Fund" the "Doing Good Fund." The name of that fund is not what makes your agency's annual fundraising efforts donor centric, how you view your donors and how you communicate with your donors is. It is just as agency-centric to ask a donor to give to the "Doing Good Fund so we can meet our income target" as it is to ask the donor to give to the "Annual Fund so we can meet our income target." The point of donor-centric fundraising is to ask donors to accomplish their goals using your agency, regardless of what your agency names its funds. I encourage nonprofits to spend their limited time and energy improving the way they view and communicate with their donors instead of renaming funds. Whatever you call your agency's "Annual Fund" it is important that it is donor centric and well run.

Because the Annual Fund cycle is timed to meet the financial needs of your agency it is by nature the least donor centric part of your agency's fundraising system. Therefore, extra care must be taken in the design of the Annual Fund to make the system as donor centric as possible. The best way to do this is to keep the donor cycle in mind. Remember that the first step in the four stage donor cycle is identification. In the Annual Fund you want to be as broad as you can possibly be when identifying new donors. This is your main source of new donor cultivation. Cast as wide of a net as you can afford to cast. The next step is cultivation. Sadly, many nonprofits skip over this stage when designing their Annual Fund. By spending a bit more money and time on cultivation in the Annual Fund the solicitation stage of your Annual Fund effort will yield better results and be more donor-centric by providing your donors with more information. The third step is what most people think of when they think of fund raising in general and Annual Fund fundraising in particular, the solicitation. Most Annual Fund solicitations are in the form of an appeal letter. Finally, the stage of Stewardship is the last stage of the donor cycle and in the annual fund traditionally consists of a thank you letter. In the next few paragraphs we will review how an agency can organize an effective, donor centric annual fund that will grow donors from qualified prospects to givers of major and planned gifts.

Let us consider Annual Fund Qualification. I have said you want to cast a broad net when qualifying prospects for your Annual Fund effort but what does that mean? For most agencies the following plan is a good one to follow when finding Annual Fund prospects. Begin by sorting all of your prospects into four different groups. Group 1: every person who has made a gift to your agency in the past three years unless you know of a valid reason to exclude them. Group 2: every person who has ever given to your nonprofit that is not included in Group 1 unless you know a valid reason to exclude them. Group 3: people who know your nonprofit personally but have not given (maybe they attended a seminar you hosted, or took a class from you, etc.) Maybe one of your donors said "add my friend Jane to your mailing list", etc. Group 4: Every person for whom you have valid contact information that is not already in group 1, 2 or 3. Lists purchased from venders go in Group 4. By building those four groups based on the above criteria you have identified and seg-mented an Annual Fund donor base.

When you are putting together your Annual Fund Plan you need to see how far down that list you can afford to go. If you have X dollars to spend, you will calculate the cost of your efforts starting with group 1 donors, then group 2 donors, then group 3 donors and then see how far down the list of group 4 donors your budget will allow you to reach. Most nonprofits find that they can afford to fully engage Groups 1 and 2 and part of group 3. They then choose to partially engage the remainder of group 3 and group 4 via cheap and less effective communication methods such as e-mail. If a donor responds to the e-mail with a gift they will move from group 4 to group 1 and be added into your agency's full Annual Fund efforts next cycle. The process of organizing your Annual Fund as described above is commonly called "seg-menting the annual fund donor base" and is an important practice to follow for optimum Annual Fund response. Segmenting your donor base based on donor's past behavior is very donor-centric because when a donor makes a gift the donor is telling the nonprofit "I have interest in your mission, linkage to your agency and the ability to give." A donor-centric fundraiser plans his or her interaction with that donor based on the information that the donor has communicated by giving. Now that your Annual Fund donor base is identified and properly segmented, let us talk about cultivation.

As I mentioned above, many nonprofits omit the donor cycle stage of cultivation in their Annual Fund efforts. They do so at their own peril. We know that the size of a donor's gift is determined by their Linkage to the agency, their Interest in the agency's mission and their Ability to make the gift. We safely assume that almost everyone we have identified has the ability to make an Annual Fund gift so in the Annual Fund we don't need to worry about Ability that much. We do need to consider Linkage and Interest. In Major Gift fundraising we work one-on-one with a donor and can therefore tailor our cultivation plan to that donor's individual needs. In the Annual Fund we do not have that luxury. Therefore our cultivation plan must be designed to raise both the Linkage and Interest of every donor in the Annual Fund campaign. The traditional (and very effective) way of doing this is by using the newsletter. It is important to cultivate using the same method that you use to solicit. Let's say you do all of your cultivation via e-mail but you send your solicitation letter using old fashioned paper mail because you know that e-mail appeals are less effective than paper appeals. Many of the donors receiving your paper solicitation do not read e-mail therefore they ONLY get your solicitation. You have not cultivated those donors at all because they never saw your e-mail newsletter. Remember, it does not matter what you said – it matters what the donor heard. As of this writing (Summer 2015) paper mail still has a MUCH higher return rate than e-mail and that shows no sign of change in the near future. Eventually, the mail appeal letter will be replaced with the monthly recurring gift from credit card or bank account as the engine of the Annual Fund. But at this point in time a nonprofit needs to do a paper appeal as part of their Annual Fund and therefore the nonprofit needs to have a paper mailing dedicated to donor cultivation that is sent to the donors it will solicit via mail appeal. Each person who receives your paper appeal letter needs to receive at least one paper cultivation mailing before he or she receives your ask letter. Ideally the cultivation mailing tells the story of your nonprofit's impact. Ideally you can send two or three cultivation mailings for every solicitation mailing. You want to appeal to the donor's interest. Use your newsletter to show your donors how your agency is already accomplishing the philanthropic goals that your donors care about. That builds the donor's interest. Next show the donor how your agency does its work well. Share a story that highlights your efficiency and professionalism. That will build on your donor's linkage. About a month after the cultivation mailing send the solicitation mailing. Tips on what makes a good solicitation letter are shared in a different section of this work. It is also very important to design your nonprofit's webpage in such a way that every person viewing it will have their interest in your work and their linkage to your agency' increased. Think of your webpage as a newsletter designed to cultivate and steward donors. A good way to do this is to highlight a story of your successful efforts to improve your world on your website's landing page. Change the story regularly. Offer hyperlinks to videos about your agency's work that you have posted on sites like YouTube. com as well as articles about your agency's impact that may appear in local newspapers or magazines. Be sure to include your recent financial statements, 990, privacy policy and other financial compliance documents in an easy to find place on your webpage. Use your webpage to tell the world that you are doing good work and doing it well. Be sure to include a donate now button, but remember the primary fundraising function of your webpage is cultivation and stewardship, not solicitation. That said, when a donor clicks "donate now" the donor should be directed to a place to immediately input his or her credit card information or PayPal password. The donor who clicks "donate now" is ready to give and does not need further cultivation information.

Stewardship is the final section of the 4 stage donor cycle. For the Annual Fund that usually means a thank you letter at the minimum. I suggest a system where volunteers such as board members make a thank you phone call to all first time donors and all gifts that are more than a certain amount established by your agency. The size of the gift that automatically triggers a special thank you phone call from a volunteer will differ from nonprofit to nonprofit depending on the size of each agency's average gift. For most nonprofits a gift of more than $500 in answer to a direct mail solicitation usually justifies a personal thank you call from a senior volunteer such as a board member. Calling first time donors with the simple purpose of saying "thank you" is a very important step for donor retention. The calls should happen within 1 business day of the agency receiving the donor's gift. As you will read in the section of this book that discusses telephone fundraising, the only time I think Annual Fund donors should be called is right after they made their gift, and the sole purpose of the call should be to say "thank you." Ideally the call should be made by a high level volunteer such as a Board Member and not an employee. The script for a thank you call might be "Mr. Smith, my name is Jane and I am a board member at NONPROFIT. I understand you just became our newest donor and I wanted to call to personally thank you. We are able to (feed the hungry, educate children, treat patients, provide clean water, etc.) only because you and others like you and I care enough to share. Your gift is appreciated." As you can tell, that is a message that can be left on a voicemail or given in person if the donor answers the call.

Thank you letters should be mailed to the donor within 1 business day of the agency receiving the donor's gift. If a donor writes you a check on Monday and you get it on Wednesday, your thank you letter should go out in the mail on Thursday, the donor should be called by a board member on Thursday (if they are a new or large donor) and on Saturday that donor should have your personal thank you letter in their hand. Within a month they should receive your next newsletter as a Stewardship mailing. Then the cycle of cultivation begins again.

Now let us look at some good tips for writing an appeal letter. First, do not use small print. Many of us cannot see small letters without straining. 12 point font is usually a good choice. You do not want to make your donors strain their eyes to read your message. Also serif font is more readable on paper and san serif font is more readable on computer screens. So, for your paper appeal letters use a serif font and for your e-mail appeals use a san serif font. Always use a font size and style that can be read easily by people with less than perfect vision. The letter should be personal. It should use "you me" language and when possible it should call the donor by name. "Dave, you and I both know that there are children who go to bed hungry in our county every night and we both think that is a needless shame. I want to tell you how you can help feed those children today. Each month *name of nonprofit* provides free food to 200 children in *name of county* through our Lunch in the Park program. Let me tell you about one of those children named Sally who I shared a sandwich with last month. . ." Because the letter is personal it should be signed. The old industry rule was to sign the letter in blue ink instead of black so that the donor could tell that it was a live signature. Of course, that worked back in the days when copy machines only made black and white copies. Today that rule has become a tradition and even though we electronically "paste" a signature in our mass printed appeal letters these days, we still say to use the color blue for the signature. I think it is wise to use a blue signature not because it makes the donor "think that someone actually signed it", our donors realize that computers print in color today, but instead because the color contrast draws the eye to the signature and reinforces the personal bond between the letter writer and the donor. That said; if you cannot afford to print your appeal letter with a blue signature do not fret about it too much. The content is more important than the color of the signature. If you have a choice, it can't hurt to use blue ink for the signature.

With the exception of the signature, I do not like the use of fake handwriting on letters. I find that at best it looks ugly and at worst is disingenuous. I find it so off putting that I personally discard all appeal letters that come to me with "fake handwriting" printed in the margin of the letter designed to look as if the author personally annotated the letter for my benefit. I feel the same way about pre-applied sticky notes affixed to the letter by the printer to look as if a person is trying to give me an "insider message." I also do not like the use of a Post Script. Many experts on appeal letters will say that the "PS is the most important part of the letter because it is the first and sometimes only thing a donor reads." I believe that the use of a key phrase or sentence strategically located under the signature is a very important part of the letter. However I find it disingenuous to call an intentionally written note a "post script." I call them "Special Note" or "Special Message" or I just write them and omit the letters "P.S." altogether.

The solicitation letter should personally connect with the donor, inform the donor of the need in the world (connecting to the donor's interest) then invite the donor to accomplish his/her philanthropic goal by making a charitable gift. The gift should be made to your agency because your agency is doing the work that your donor cares about and is doing it well (linkage). The letter should reiterate the specific request you are making of the donor at least three times including in the portion of the letter that is below the signature. Avoid calling that final note a "PS" unless you literally hand write it after you have personally signed the letter (the definition of a post script). Instead simply call that last call to action a "Special Message."

Do not try to cultivate or steward the donor in the solicitation letter. Those are separate steps in the 4 stage donor cycle and should be performed separately. Of course if the letter is going to a person who has given in the past, it is appropriate and sometimes necessary to acknowledge that giving. Saying "Your long time support has made our community better in countless ways. Your gift of $50 today will ensure that the senior citizens of our community have the resource center they need to live full and productive lives." is certainly appropriate in a solicitation letter. Saying "Please accept our thanks in advance for the gift we know you will make." is not acceptable. Honor the donor's right to think for him or herself and then thank the donor properly if he or she chooses to share.

You have the giving history for your group one and group two donors in your files. Therefore you can use that data to ask the donors in those two Annual Fund segments for a specific gift amount and you should do so. The rule I use for Annual Fund ask amounts is as follows; if the donor has given once before I specifically ask that donor for a gift of the same amount as he or she gave last time. For instance, if the donor gave one gift in the past and that gift was $10 then I ask that donor for $10 this time. If the donor has given more than one gift and the donor's last two gifts were of different amounts then I ask for the higher of their last two gift amounts. For instance if the donor gave a gift of $10 one time and a gift of $15 at another time then I would ask that donor for $15 this time. If the donor has given two times or more and that donor's last two gifts were of the same value, then I ask that donor for an increased gift. For instance, if he gave $15 and $15 then I would ask him to give $20 this time. This plan for increasing the size of gifts over time by asking for specific gift amounts based on the donor's past giving history is called "moves management." It embodies the mantra of the Annual Fund that is "Get the Gift. Repeat the Gift. Upgrade the Gift." A good moves management plan requires keeping good records in your database about your donor's giving patterns. You must be able to get these numbers out of your database and into a spread sheet that can be mail merged into your appeal letters. Many nonprofits fail to do good moves management work simply because their data collection systems are inadequate. If your current database system does not allow for the moves management system described above, you must improve that system before you can reach your annual fund's potential with moves management. If you fail to reach your annual fund's potential through moves management you will not grow major donors because Major Gifts grow out of the Annual Fund's moves management system. When a donor's giving reaches a certain point through your Annual Fund giving (an amount that will be determined by each nonprofit) then that donor should be considered a Major Gift prospect and treated accordingly as part of the agency's Major Gift program as described in a different section of this work. Personally, I like to look for donors who are consistently giving $1,000 or more to the Annual fund each year and donors who have a cumulative life time total giving of $10,000 or more to my nonprofit and consider them as Major Gift Prospects. This is how a donor-centric nonprofit grows its pool of Major Gift prospects.

The final stage of the donor cycle is Stewardship. At its most basic level stewardship consists of saying thank you. As mentioned above, thank you phone calls and thank you letters should take place within 1 business day of the agency receiving the donor's gift. I have frequently heard agencies say that they do not have the ability to respond that quickly. Those agencies will never reach their full potential and the mission they have been established to meet will not met as effectively as it could be if the nonprofit took a more donor-centric approach to stewardship. That is unfortunate and easily fixable. Just as you would not invite 50 people over to dinner if you only have a dining room table for 8, you should not send out 5000 letters expecting a 10 percent rate of return if you do not have the internal capacity to send out 500 thank you letters within 24 hours. Instead of sending out all 5000 letters at once, send them out in small batches that you can handle. Just as I would not invite all 50 of my friends over for dinner on the same night, but rather over the course of the year each of my friends may be invited to my home for dinner once or twice. To know how many letters you should send at once you need to know your agency's average rate of return for mail appeal. As discussed in the Metrics chapter of this book, your agency must track this data to reach your maximum level of success. This is an example of why that data is important and how it can be used to ensure your fundraising efforts are donor-centric by thanking your donors promptly. If you are at the point where even spreading your mail appeal out over time will not allow you to respond to your gifts appropriately it is time to inspect your gift receiving process to ensure it is moving as fast and efficiently as possible, and next to add manpower to that part of the operation. If you cannot afford more staff, get volunteers to help, this is a great way for a board member who says "I am not a fundraiser" to be positively involved in the fundraising process. Making sure we thank our donors within 24 hours is a very important part of fundraising. Many nonprofits can spread their mail appeals out over the year except for their end of year mailing that is sent to every donor and prospect in group 1, group 2, group 3 and maybe even group 4. A nonprofit in that situation needs to use its volunteer base to thank donors at the time of end of the year appeal but be able to use staff for the rest of the year.

The thank you letter should be brief and clear. It should call the donor by name and thank him or her for the personal gift that was just made by specifying the amount of the gift and then informing the donor of how that gift will make the world better. "Dave, in today's mail I received your check for $50.00. Your gift will provide meals for 20 children who would have otherwise went hungry. On behalf of each of those children whose nutritional needs you have met – THANK YOU." While I think it is acceptable to use a preprinted signature on your appeal letter, I believe each thank you letter should be personally signed with a hand written note of thanks to the donor. Here is where it really does help to use a distinctive ink, such as blue ink for your signature. However, since blue ink can be used in today's copy machines, I take the additional personal touch of signing my name using a fountain pen filled with bright blue ink. That way it is clear to anyone that I actually did sign the letter. The little ink smudges and smears that only a fountain pen produce make that evident. I want my donors to know that they are valued enough that their gifts are personally appreciated and will make our world better.

When donors give online they should receive an automatic email at the moment of their gift acknowledging receipt and saying thank you. Everyone knows this is automatic. Donors like to see it because it assures them that the gift was made and their credit card was processed. But it DOES NOT COUNT AS A THANK YOU NOTE. The point of a thank you letter is to make the donor feel PERSONALLY APPRECIATED that is something an automated e-mail, no matter how well written cannot accomplish. Do send the automatic e-mail, but ALSO send the real thank you letter within 24 hours.

DO NOT SOLICIT the donor for another gift in the thank you letter. Do not even try to CULTIVATE the donor for another gift in the thank you letter. Remember each of those important tasks take place at a different stage of the 4 step fundraising cycle. This is the time to STEWARD and thank. Assuming you are in the United States and that your donor did not receive any goods or services in exchange for his or her gift, you should indicate that in the letter. I like to put that detail in a foot note using the smallest type size that is readable. That is not the main point of the letter and I do not want it to distract from the main point of the letter which is to make the donor feel good about his choice and feel that his choice has accomplished his philanthropic goal. Just put that little statement in small print at the bottom of the letter to keep the donor's CPA happy.

A healthy annual fund system will likely consist of several direct mailings throughout the year. Your nonprofit will likely always be in the middle of one of those mailings to a different group of donors. You can plan these mailings to provide your agency with income at the time of year that the income is needed. Knowing your average rate of return and your average gift size allows you to control how much money you will receive and when that money will be received. At this point in time, direct mail is still the engine of the Annual Fund but it is not ALL of the Annual Fund.

The future of the Annual Fund is the automatic monthly gift made from the donor's credit card or bank account. Just a few years ago only the biggest nonprofits could accept gifts made with a credit card. Today anyone with an iPhone can do so. Donors expect you to be able to take their credit card gift. Your annual fund appeal letters must have a way for donors to write their credit card number on the remit slip and it should give your agency's webpage address so donors can read your mail appeal letter and go online to give. Your direct mail appeal should also encourage donors to sign up for your recurring giving program by going to your webpage and signing up to give a specific amount each month from their credit card or bank account. Technology to-day allows you to include a special URL in your mail appeal letter. When donors type that URL into their browser they will go to your webpage in a way that allows you to measure how many donors came to your webpage as a result of reading your mail appeal letter. This data can be tracked and used to count the gifts that are made this way as part of your Mail Appeal campaign's success.

According to the M+R 2015 Benchmarks Report 17% of nonprofit in-come came in through a monthly recurring giving program of some sort in 2014. I believe that the monthly recurring "automatic-giving" program linked to good online webpage content will someday replace the direct mail appeal letter as the engine of the Annual Fund.

When a donor signs up for the nonprofit's "auto giving program" that do-nor should be removed them from the normal direct mail plan. Ensure that those donors continue to get your newsletters mailed to them and special post cards sent to them that say "THANK YOU" for your monthly giving. That postcard should have a web link for them to go to view examples of the good work that their regular giving is doing in the world. I want each "automatic monthly giver" to be in a special direct mail program designed just for them. Each donor who is an automatic monthly-giver should get 4 mailings per year. Namely; two newsletters and two thank you post cards that offer the donor the opportunity to go to a webpage designed to showcase the agency's good work. The "automatic-giver" should also get one mail appeal letter at the end of the calendar year. It should be a special mailing that only "auto givers" receive. The letter should thank the donor for his or her giving. It should clearly state the amount that the donor gives each month and the length of time that the donor has a monthly automatic giver. The letter should inform the donor that if he or she does not respond to that mailing, the nonprofit will continue to charge the donor's credit card at the same amount each month until the donor tells the nonprofit to stop doing so. This should be communicated in a positive way such as "We will continue to accept your generous monthly gift of $10.00 which will be used to feed the homeless in our town. Knowing we can depend upon your gift each month ensures that our mission to feed the hungry is accomplished. If at any time you would like to change the value of your monthly gift simply let us know." The letter should encourage the donor to keep his or her contact information current with the nonprofit. If the "Automatic giver" has been giving the same monthly amount for 2 years or more, then that donor's letter should ask that donor to increase his or her monthly auto giving amount. I usually ask for an increase of 25% rounded to the nearest whole dollar. For instance, if the donor has been giving $10 per month for the past two years, that donor should be asked to give $13 per month. If the donor does not reply to the mailing that donor's monthly gift amount will stay $10.00. If that donor replies by checking the box that says "Yes, I will do even more good in our world by increasing my monthly gift to $13" then his gift increases and he should be thanked with a letter for his new recurring monthly gift of $13 per month. That letter should be sent within 1 business day of when you received his letter saying he would increase his gift. If the donor wants to stop giving to your agency he will contact you using the contact information you provide in the letter. This is the best method to ensure good moves management and donor retention in the automatic giving program.

It is important that the system you chose to handle your "automatic giving" program automatically keeps track of credit card expiration dates and automatically e-mails your donors 2 months before their credit card is scheduled to expire with a link that the donor can click on to update his credit card information so that giving can go on uninterrupted. The procedure I suggest is that your system should automatically email the donor 2 months before expiration and if no action has been taken by the donor then the system automatically e-mails the donor again 1 month before the expiration date. If no action has been taken within 2 weeks of the expiration date then the system should e-mail your development staff. Your development staff should then generate a paper mailing to the donor thanking him for his giving and reminding him that his credit card will soon expire. Encourage him to fill out the enclosed form and return it to you with his new credit card number. This is the only instance where I use a Self-Addressed Stamped Envelope as the remit envelope in Annual Fund work. In this case I want to make it as easy as possible for a donor to update his information. At this point the donor has not updated his credit card information after getting 2 e-mails (assuming his e-mail is working) so that action has communicated to me that he needs an even easier way to update his information. I want to make it as easy as possible on this guy. All he needs to do is fill out the form and drop it in the mail. If that letter goes unanswered and the card expires. I suggest a phone call as a last ditch effort. If that is unfruitful, the donor should be sent a letter thanking him for his membership in the "auto giving club" and inviting him to return to that club at any time by simply going to your webpage. I would then consider that donor a group 1 donor in your annual fund mail appeal list. The nonprofit's system should allow donors to log on to your webpage and change/update their credit card information whenever they want to. As our society experiences more and more "data breeches" that result in credit card numbers changing frequently this is very important. Many donors will find themselves needing to update their credit card information with your automatic giving program several times in any given year as they receive new credit card numbers due to data breeches. You must make this process as easy as possible for your donors if you want your automatic giving program to succeed at its fullest potential. With today's technology a nonprofit's webpage; database and e-mail communication systems can all be fully integrated with your credit card processing system to allow the system I described above to give your donors the best possible service.

Many nonprofits use a telethon as part of their Annual Fund effort. While this used to be a very popular method of fundraising within the Annual Fund system, today it is a technique I personally advise against. Years ago our telephones were bolted to the wall of our kitchens. This ensured that if we were speaking on the phone we were in a comfortable place. Because you controlled what time you made the phone call to your donor, you could always be assured that if the donor answered the call he was in a comfortable place at a reasonable time. If the donor was busy laying under his car trying to get a jammed oil filter off with a wrench that was bent because his son ran it over with a bicycle, then the phone rang in an empty home and the donor did not know about it, unless he had an answering machine and later heard a nice message from his beloved nonprofit when he was done working on the car and came inside. Then he could choose to delete the message or call back at a time that worked for him. Today, we carry our phones with us EVERYWHERE. If you called that same donor today at the same time, he would be under his car fighting that stuck oil filter with the bent wrench when his pocket started to vibrate. Then his attempt to get the phone out of his pocket would cause him to drop the wrench on the ground and bang his head on the exhaust pipe of the car he was under, the Dixie land band ring tone would get louder and louder as his annoyance level increased. To stop the phone from making noise he would stick his greasy hand into his pocket to answer it. "Hello" he will finally gasp into the phone while lying on his back, head bruised, phone greasy, heavily annoyed, oil dripping on his garage floor from a half removed filter that he is helplessly staring at while he talks on the phone. The cellphone signal is choppy and he has to strain to hear the person on the other end. Now he is annoyed, uncomfortable and angry. The first words he hears in that position and frame of mind is the name of your nonprofit. That is not how we want to interact with our donors. Yet, if we randomly call a list of donors today we are likely to find many donors in a position like that. Also, many donors have cell phone plans that charge them money to receive calls. Of course, these problems would not happen if we all turned off our phones when we were not in a position to answer them. But honestly, most of us don't do that. When is the last time you sat through a movie or even a staff meeting without someone's phone buzzing? Furthermore, today the phone is being used more for texting than it is for talking. People, especially younger people, leave their phones on because they want to get texts and then they get annoyed when an actual phone call comes in from someone other than a close friend or family member. For this reason I have no problem with a nonprofit sending out Thank you texts to its donors or even a text based fundraising campaign asking donors to click a link to give, but I do not think using the phone in Annual Fund solicitation makes sense now that cellphones are king. You may think you are calling the donor's home number because the number is labeled as "home" in your database, but more and more people only have cellphones these days and so they list their cellphone number on the "home" line when they fill out a form. If you are going to use a telephone campaign as part of your Annual Fund against my advice then I highly suggest doing a telephone thank you campaign instead of a solicitation campaign. If a donor gets a call at an awkward time or place, just hearing you say "thank you" will likely not upset him or her as much as if you are asking for a financial gift. As discussed above, a thank you call to new or large donors made within 24 hours of receiving their gift is the only time I believe making a phone call to an Annual Fund donor does more good than harm as a general rule. Remember, most of the people in your Annual Fund pool are not people with extremely high linkage or interest. If they were, you would already be cultivating them for a Major Gift with a one-on-one strategy not calling them as part of your Annual Fund drive. Even if your agency does include your major donors in its annual fund drive, those donors will still be the minority of the donors in your Annual Fund pool. It is becoming a growing practice to send all donors in the telephone campaign a postcard before the phone call date to allow the donors the option of opting out of the campaign by making a gift before the telephone campaign starts or by simply telling the nonprofit they do not wish to be called. This practice is growing among higher education alumni fundraisers because alumni fundraising is one of the few sectors of the nonprofit world where the telephone campaign is still being widely used. While I like the concept, I think it is just easier to do a postcard campaign to start with and forget about making unsolicited phone calls to your Annual Fund donors.

Instead of a phone campaign, consider a postcard campaign. I think post-cards are a great tool in the Annual Fund. I use them for both Cultivation and Stewardship purposes. Each Thanksgiving send all of the donors who will receive a solicitation from you in the coming year a big postcard that says "During this season of thanksgiving we are thankful for you." At other times during the year send your donors a postcard that briefly highlights some of your agency's work. Put a webpage address on the post card where donors can go to learn more. If you use a special URL for that purpose you can measure how many donors visit the webpage as a result of reading your postcard. The post card has three major advantages in the world of direct mail. First, it is cheaper than sending a letter. Second, a well-designed post card is visually appealing, engaging and "cool." I have seen people put postcards up on their refrigerators and cork boards because they liked how the card looked and were inspired by its message. Finally, the best strength of the postcard is that the postcard has to be read by everyone who touches it! There is an old saying in the direct mail business that "the most important part of your direct mail piece is the envelope because that is the only part that your donor HAS to read." The idea behind that statement is that there should be some message on the envelope that makes the donor want to open the letter to read more. With the postcard, everyone who touches it has to read it whether they want to or not. There is no envelope that needs to be opened to see your message. Even if all a person does is take your postcard from their mail box to their trash can, they will have read your message, at least in large part. One non-profit I worked with used to create elaborate annual reports and send them to every donor. This was a great stewardship and cultivation practice. However it was also very expensive. We modified that method by creating a special annual report postcard that was much cheaper to print and mail than the full annual report. The post card was sent to everyone who used to get the Annual Report. The post card hit the main points of the Annual Report and then directed readers to a special webpage where they could view a digital annual report that had videos and interactive sections. That moved the agency into the future and made better use of its limited fundraising budget. The postcard is a powerful tool in the donor-centric Annual Fund fundraising effort.

E-mail has a very small role to play in Annual Fund fundraising. If it were not such a cheap communication medium it would have no place at all. Every study I have read about gifts made as a direct result of an e-mail campaign shows email to be a SIGNIFICANTLY poorer performer than standard mail appeal letters for Annual Fund Fundraising. I think we should send our donor's electronic newsletters in addition to the paper newsletters. A good practice is to send a quarterly paper newsletter and a monthly e-newsletter. I think we should use social media to communicate the good programmatic work that our agency is doing. Major Gift Officers should use e-mail when personally communicating with a specific donor. However, in the Annual Fund, statistics show that little is gained from electronic mass appeal e-mails. That said, because it is very inexpensive to do an electronic appeal, it is a good idea to use e-mail for this purpose for segment 4 of the Annual Fund donor base who would otherwise have went unreached. Just don't expect earth shattering results. I have had people tell me that their e-mail campaign was successful. I have followed that up by saying that their nonprofit's appeal would have been even more successful if they had used paper. According to the 2015 M+R Benchmark Report[1], the average fundraising response rate for an e-mail appeal in 2014 was only 0.06%. Compare that to the typical paper mail return rate of 5% and you can see why I say that you should use paper instead of e-mail for your appeal work. That same report shows that the average nonprofit's e-mail list grew by 14 percent in 2014. That means nonprofits are sending more e-mail than ever. The fact that all of us are receiving more e-mail messages than ever before is a good reason to avoid using e-mail as a fundraising vehicle. Think about it, how many e-mail accounts do you have? I actively monitor five accounts. I check each one about 20 times a day which is basically every time I glance at my phone. I pay serious attention to three of those five accounts. The two accounts I don't monitor closely are mainly used when I am required to submit an e-mail address as part of a transaction or to receive a coupon or discount code. I have two such accounts because some web pages and services have started requiring two different e-mail addresses to register to use them. I read everything that comes to my work account unless it is obviously spam. If a nonprofit adds that e-mail address to their mailing list

I unsubscribe. My work e-mail account is too important to receive anything except messages directly related to my work. I tell my e-mail system that any mass e-mail received to that account that does not come from my employer is spam. It is possible that nonprofits are sending me messages at that address and that I never see because of my spam filtering. For the other two accounts that I monitor throughout the day, I read the subject line of every e-mail I receive. I delete most of them without ever reading the actual e-mail content. I get over 200 messages per day on average. I can't read every e-mail and still have time to do anything else. My relationship with e-mail is not unusual. Every day when I come home from work I stop at the mail box and carry the mail in. I set it down on the kitchen counter and sort it. Mail for my spouse goes in one pile, mail I want to read later goes in another. Advertisements and catalogues usually gets glanced at, and then thrown into the trash can next to the counter. Anything that looks exciting or urgent gets opened and read on the spot. That usually includes any personal letter and anything that appears official (such as letters from my insurance agent or my doctor's office). On any given day my family receives an average of 5 to 10 items in our mail box. My e-mail alone has more than 200 messages. If you are competing for attention in our household, you do better to compete against the 4 to 9 other letters I have in my hand coming home from the mail box than against the literal HUNDREDS of e-mails that are processed throughout the day between my spouse and I. Of course most e-mail is now read on mobile devices so if an e-mail is not formatted for easy reading on my phone I get annoyed and delete it unread, even though the computer metric system that the sender is using to monitor the open rate will tell the sender that I opened the message because it did download to my phone.

Whether I read an e-mail or not depends on what I am doing when I see it in my inbox. If an e-mail that looks moderately interesting hits when I am just trying to get through my inbox before my next meeting, I will delete it unread. Again, from talking with others I know I am not alone in my treatment of e-mail.

If you send me a letter, you know that I am going to be in the comfort of my front yard when I first interact with your letter at my mailbox.

Furthermore it will be at a time I have chosen to get my mail. If your e-mail hits my mobile phone while I was in the middle of something else, I may just delete it unread to stop my phone from blinking. A donor-centric approach to communication chooses to use the method that the agency's donor base is most likely to appreciate and respond to, not just the method that is cheapest and easiest for the nonprofit to use. Give serious consideration to how your donors view e-mail and how they view written letters. If your donors are like me, and like most Americans, you will do well to choose paper over electronic communication in your donor-centric Annual Fund efforts.

So, is there a use for mass e-mail campaigns in the Annual Fund? Yes. I suggest that about a week after every direct mail is sent, that you send an e-mail version of the letter to the donors to whom it was mailed, as well as your group 4 donors who you are only able to afford to communicate with via e-mail. The email should explain that they may have received a copy of this letter in the mail already. It should also say that if they have already responded to that letter their generosity is appreciated but if they have not yet heard this message or responded, now is a good time to take action on one of their philan-thropic priorities. A clickable link should be in the ask section of the e-mail saying "CLICK HERE to give now." Because most e-mail is read on mobile devices and people may read their e-mail in a place where they do not want to take out their credit card, consider using a PayPal button on e-mail appeals. This will allow your donors to give by simply typing in their PayPal password instead of pulling out their wallet while they are on the train home from work.

The e-mail solicitation should ask the donor for the same amount that your paper mail asked that donor for. Many nonprofits keep two lists. One list from their database tied to donor records that they use for paper appeals and another list in their e-mail service that they use for e-mail appeals. That is not a good practice. It leads to confusion and duplication. Your e-mail appeal list should be the same as your paper mail list and should be generated by your database and contain an ask amount that is donor-centric based on the donor's giving history. The e-mail appeal letter's ask should be the same as the paper appeal letter that the donor received in the mail. Because people can have more than one e-mail address you cannot de-dupe your database mailing list against the list you have in your e-mail server effectively. You cannot know if the John Smith in your database who has the e-mail address John.Smith@aol.com and is a strong donor is the same John Smith in your e-mail list whose e-mail in that file is listed as Grandpajohn@juno.com or if they are two different people. You do not know what to ask that person for. Is he the John Smith who is a long time donor or is he a new prospect? Use one master list tied to donor giving history from your database for both your paper and electronic mail appeal work and this problem will be avoided. Using one master list for all appeals will allow you to ask the donor for the same amount in the email as well as in the paper letter.

Use e-mail as a follow up to mail appeal letters and also include group 4 segment Annual Fund prospects in your e-mail solicitations if it is the only way you reach them and is the best you can afford for that group of prospects.

Online giving is growing, but not thanks to e-mail appeals. Donors are getting print appeal letters and going online. They are also viewing the webpages of nonprofit agencies and then clicking the donate button because the message communicated in the webpage aligns with the donor's philanthropic priorities.

"Social Media" is the current buzzword in fundraising circles. This, in spite of the fact that very little money is actually being raised through social media campaigns. Using social media outlets such as Facebook and Twitter to inform a donor base about the work your agency is doing is a good practice. This alone is not enough, however. It is hard to target messages using social media and the messages must be very brief. That said, when your webpage is updated with your newest story of impact, it is a good idea to tweet about it and post a link to the story on your nonprofit's Facebook page. These acts will build linkage and possibly interest among your donor base. Social Media can play a role in your Annual Fund's cultivation plan in this way. It cannot be the only part of your Annual Fund's cultivation plan and it cannot serve as the solicitation part of your Annual Fund's plan. You can generally thank donors with broad statements of thanks using social media but you cannot steward a personal gift using social media. Therefore social media can play a small role in your Annual Fund's stewardship plan, but cannot replace the personal thank you, or the thank you letter. Social media should best be viewed as an extension of your newsletter and as a tool to drive traffic to your webpage. Social Media can be a small part of a nonprofit's Annual Fund cultivation and stewardship activities. Depending on the nature of your nonprofit's work, social media may play a large role in your programmatic work. This is especially true for advocacy nonprofits that exist to mobilize volunteers for political impact. This programmatic use of social media must not be confused with fundraising. However, as the agency's volunteers engage with the agency to take action after being inspired by the agency's social media message, their linkage and interest will improve, thus showing that social media can indeed be part of an agency's cultivation and stewardship plan. However, social media cannot rightly be used for solicitation as it is impossible to personalize a solicitation message on Facebook or Twitter or to share the message in a private way. A general ask can be made, but that is not donor-centric and is not a best practice. Even so called private messages sent over Facebook Messenger are legally owned by Facebook. Sharing donor information using that medium would therefore violate the privacy policy of any well run nonprofit because by sharing the donor's personal information over Facebook messenger, the nonprofit would be sharing that information with Facebook. Similarly, a nonprofit cannot use g-mail or any other webmail service that scans and reads outgoing e-mail to share such information for the same reason. Because social media cannot be used for all parts of the donor cycle, it is impossible to have a true "social media fundraising campaign." Social media can only be part of a fundraising campaign when it is used as one of many ways to cultivate and steward gifts.

A healthy Annual Fund will consist of several mail appeals throughout the year and an ongoing "auto giving credit card" program. Everyone in your Annual Fund's Donor pool will receive special cultivation communications sent in the format that you are sending their solicitation prior to any solicitation being sent. All donors will be thanked for their gift within 1 business day of your agency receiving their gift via a personal letter and new donors and donors who give large gifts will also receive a personal thank you phone call from a volunteer within 24 hours of your agency receiving the gift. The messaging in your Annual Fund appeals will be donor-centric, meaning it will inform the donor about the work your agency does that aligns with the donor's personal philanthropic goals. You will then invite the donor to accomplish her or his philanthropic goal by making a gift to your nonprofit because your nonprofit will effectively and efficiently use that gift to accomplish the donor's goal. You will then communicate the impact that the donor's gift had in the world to that donor in a way that is meaningful to the donor.

THE ANNUAL FUND AND MAJOR/PLANNED GIFTS

Many nonprofit leaders ask me "How do I find Major Gift prospects for my agency?" Many nonprofits pay large sums of money to companies who do "wealth screenings" and will provide the nonprofit with a list containing the names and contact information for people who the company says have high net-worth and give to charity. This is a common way for a nonprofit to fail in its Major Gifts effort. Major Donors are not imported to an agency; they are grown from within that agency's Annual Fund.

Earlier we discussed the idea that every donor has Interest in your agency's mission, Linkage to your specific nonprofit and the Ability to make a gift. A donor's giving will not rise above the lowest of those three metrics. A donor may have high ability and high interest but does not know your agency exists. Such a person will not make a gift to your agency due to lack of linkage. Your Annual Fund system identifies a wide range of prospective donors and then cultivates them by intentionally working to raise their interest in your mission and linkage to your agency. Your Annual Fund then solicits a gift that is the appropriate size based on that donor's history of giving. Your agency then thanks the donor promptly and informs the donor of the impact his or her most recent gift had. That builds the donor's linkage. Your donor receives information about the good work your agency is doing to accomplish your mission, most likely in the form of newsletters. That increases interest. Then you solicit another gift, because the donor's interest and linkage have gone up due to the design of your Annual Fund, the gift size of your donor will increase over time as well. When a donor starts making frequent large gifts in response to your Annual Fund it is time for your Major Gift Officer to reach out to that donor as a Major/Planned gift prospect. The size of the donor's gift that put the donor on the MGO's RADAR will vary from agency to agency but for most agencies, a donor who frequently gives $1000 gifts in response to an Annual Fund appeal should be considered a Major Gift prospect. This is the best way to get Major Gift Prospects. The Major Gift section of this book discusses how the Major Gifts Officer will cultivate, solicit and steward these donors. Some nonprofits say "but we don't have any donors like that yet" or "we don't know if we have any donors like that because we do not keep good records." To those nonprofits I say you are not yet ready to do major gift work. Get your Annual Fund in order first. Remember nonprofits do not exist to receive gifts. Donors give THROUGH nonprofits to accomplish their personal philanthropic goals. Your nonprofit must be able to effectively, efficiently and sustainably accomplish the philanthropic goals of the donor before you have the moral right to ask your donor to make a gift of accumulated wealth and a large part of being able to do that is keeping good records and treating your donor base in a donor-centric way through a well-run Annual Fund.

There is a kind of planned gift prospect who will show up in your Annual Fund in a different way. This is the donor who has high interest in your agency's mission and high linkage to your agency but relatively low ability. The cap that will stop this person's gift size from continually increasing is ability. These donors interest will continue to grow and their linkage will continue to grow as you interact with them through your Annual Fund system. However because their ability is not growing their annual fund gift will not increase in size. These are the people who will answer every mail appeal you send to them with a gift that is the same size as they gave last time. They always give and their gift stays the same size. They are excellent Bequest prospects. Ideally, you will reach out to them as you would any major donor, one-on-one to thank them for their long history of giving and in a one-on-one setting you will inform them about how they can accomplish their philanthropic goal with a bequest to your nonprofit. Some agencies have so many donors like this that they are not able to reach out to all of them in a one-on-one way as they would do in an ideal world so they send these donors a special mailing about bequest giving.

These donors are usually thrilled to learn that they can have the philanthropic impact that they never thought they could have. Most people do not realize the power of a charitable bequest. Many people "feel poor" and so do not think about what they could do if they planned their giving. Many people think "I do not have much so I do not need a will." Many people do not itemize their taxes, have modest income and so they do not think about the fact that in the year of their death, the balance of their tax advantaged retirement account will be received by their estate as ordinary income and make their federal income tax liability almost 40% that year. They are happy to learn that by making your charity the beneficiary of part of their 401K plan they can send that money to your nonprofit instead of to the government. I have honestly had many donors like this come to tears when we met and they realized that they "could make a big difference after all." To me, that is what being a gift officer is about – we are here to help donor's use the resources they have to best accomplish their philanthropic goals.

Chapter 8

RESOURCE SAMPLES

RESOURCE ONE

SAMPLE BOARD MEMBER
JOB DESCREPTION & COMMITMENT FORM

NAME OF NONPROFIT is a 501(c)3 non-profit corporation of the state of STATE. The mission of NAME OF NONPROFIT is MISSION STATEMENT.

TERM:

3 years, expiring after the installation of successor. Terms are renewable at request of the nominating committee until term limit is reached. Specific details contained in NAME OF NONPROFIT' by-laws.

RESPONSIBILITIES:

1. Endorse and uphold the mission of NAME OF NONPROFIT
2. Contribute to the creation of long-range plans and fundraising goals.
3. Raise funds for NAME OF NONPROFIT through direct solicitation involvement

4. Provide ultimate oversight of NAME OF NONPROFIT as a fiduciary for NAME OF NONPROFIT make decisions with personal honesty and integrity in the best interests of NAME OF NONPROFIT.
5. Ensure that NAME OF NONPROFIT is a responsible steward of resources
6. Review and approve NAME OF NONPROFIT's budget and policies
7. Contribute to the enhancement NAME OF NONPROFIT's public image

OBLIGATIONS:

1. Board members are expected to make a personally significant annual financial contribution to NAME OF NONPROFIT. NAME OF NONPROFIT encourages Board members to consider their gift to NAME OF NONPROFIT to be their primary charitable contribution excluding gifts to their religious community while they are on the Board of Directors.*
2. Board members are expected to attend all Board meetings unless excused by the Board President. The Board meets every other month. Meeting locations and times are communicated via e-mail. A schedule of board meetings for the next 12 months is attached to this document. ATTACH BOARD METING SCHEDULE.
3. Every Board member will be asked by the President to serve on a Board Committee. Active participation in that committee's work is expected. Requests for appointment to a specific committee may be made to the Board President.
4. Lend one's name, expertise and credibility to the fundraising activities of NAME OF NONPROFIT
5. Identify, cultivate and recruit Board members and other volunteers
6. Help identify potential donors and assist in the cultivation, solicitation and stewardship of donors with the assistance and guidance of NAME OF NONPROFIT's staff

7. Attend NAME OF NONPROFIT's special events such as the agency's annual dinner and open house event. The dates of these events are INSERT DATES, TIMES AND LOCATIONS.

8. Agree to disclose any existing or potential conflict(s) of interest and recuse him/herself from voting on issues for which a current conflict exists.

9. The NAME OF NONPROFIT Board encourages open dialogue and full discussion of all matters before the Board, taking all viewpoints into consideration. Once the Board resolves a decision through voting, all Board Members agree to speak with one voice and honor confidentiality of Board decisions.

*In general: while serving on the Board, NAME OF NONPROFIT should be at the top of your philanthropic giving list each year. One rule of thumb is to make your gift to NAME OF NONPROFIT second only to your donation to your faith community. Taking into account profession, length of time in the occupation, differences in salaries and other factors, some Board Members will be able to give more than others. NAME OF NONPROFIT asks you to make a gift of personal significance for you – whatever that amount may be.

BOARD MEMBER YEARLY GOALS:

1. My personal "Annual Giving" goal this year is*: _____
   - I will make/have made a 3 year pledge of $_____
   - I would like to talk with NAME OF NONPROFIT's development officer to discuss a planned gift (bequest, life income agreement, etc.)

2. My Personal "Getting Goal": As a Board Member I agree to participate when called upon to: A. Make at least 3 fundraising visits for NAME OF NONPROFIT including:
   - Cultivation Visits
   - Solicitation Visits
   - Stewardship Visits

3. I will help identify 3 new donors for CCR

4. I will attend all Board Meetings as called. If I am unable to attend I will inform the Board President as soon as possible.

5. I will attend the NAME OF NONPROFIT's Annual Dinner and other public events as far as possible. If I am unable to attend I will inform the organizer of the event as soon as possible.

6. I will actively participate on the committee to which I am assigned. If I am unable to fulfill the obligations of my committee I will inform the committee chair as soon as possible.

7. I will honor all NAME OF NONPROFIT's policies and procedures

Signed:_____

Date:_____

RESOURCE TWO

SAMPLE GIFT ACCEPTANCE POLICY FOR SMALL OR MEDIUM NONPROFIT NOT EQUPITED TO OFFER CGA'S OR SERVE AS TRUSTEE OF TRUSTS

These gift acceptance policies have been adopted by the NAME OF NONPROFIT Board of Directors on DATE to govern the receipt of all financial contributions to the organization, including gifts donated through estate, legacy or planned giving.

A. Estate, Legacy or Planned Giving

The term, planned giving, is used generically in this document to refer to financial gifts made through what is commonly referred to as estate, legacy or planned giving. Planned Giving is a comprehensive program for long-term financial support of NAME OF NONPROFIT through a broad range of charitable gift options. The program actively solicits and accepts contributions to NAME OF NONPROFIT through bequests and other advantageous tax, financial, and estate planning techniques. The following policies and procedures are adopted as guidelines to clarify the technical aspects of receiving and managing gifts.

B. Types of Gifts Accepted

1. *Cash and Marketable Securities.* Outright gifts of cash and marketable securities may be accepted by the NAME OF NONPROFIT Executive Director and/or his/her designee.
2. *Life Insurance.* Gifts of whole life insurance when NAME OF NONPROFIT is designated as beneficiary or both owner and beneficiary may be accepted by the Executive Director or his/her designee. When all the rights in a policy are gifted to NAME OF NONPROFIT, the donor shall

be informed of the advantages of making a gift of the premium amount to NAME OF NONPROFIT and encouraged to continue to make the premium payments.

3. *Tangible Personal Property.* Gifts of tangible personal property may be accepted by the Executive Director or his/her designee.

4. *Closely-Held Business Stock.* Gifts of closely held stock when given outright, given to fund a charitable trust for which NAME OF NONPROFIT will serve as trustee, given in exchange for a gift annuity, or given as an in-kind distribution from a trust or estate require prior approval of the Fund Development Committee.

5. *Limited partnership Interests.* Gifts of limited partnership interests when given outright, given to fund a charitable trust of which NAME OF NONPROFIT is the beneficiary, given in exchange for a gift annuity, or given as an in-kind distribution from a trust or estate require prior approval of the Fund Development Committee. Unrelated business income must be estimated and evaluated for each partnership.

6. *Real Property.* Gifts of real estate when given outright, given to fund a charitable trust, given in exchange for a gift annuity, or given as an in-kind distribution from a trust or estate require prior approval of the Fund Development Committee. The Fund Development Committee Chairperson and the Executive Director shall summarize the following information and present it with a recommendation for acceptance or non-acceptance to the Fund Development Committee.

   a. On-Site Inspection Report. One or more representatives of NAME OF NONPROFIT shall make an on-site inspection of the property and prepare a written report. NAME OF NONPROFIT may retain a licensed contractor to inspect the property.

b. Analysis of Marketability, Holding Costs, and Costs of Sale. The Executive Director or his/her designee shall evaluate the net holding costs, if any, and prospective sales costs of the property. Criteria for evaluation shall include:

- present market value, including obtaining a formal appraisal
- marketability - assessment of the market for salability, including likely timeframe for sale
- cost of acquisition
- income potential while the property is held
- encumbrances
- zoning
- appreciation/depreciation potential
- maintenance and repair expense
- loan expense
- property tax, unrelated income tax, and other taxes
- marketing, commission and closing costs
- improvement, renovation, or retrofitting

When real property is used to fund a charitable trust for which NAME OF NONPROFIT will be a beneficiary, the donor must make arrangements with an independent legal or financial contractor to manage all aspects of the trust, including all expenses incurred prior to any sale of the property, including the cost of environmental assessments described below.

c. *Hazardous Materials and Environmental Issues.* NAME OF NONPROFIT shall carefully investigate environmental issues related to the property. For residential property only, where no environmental problems are found or suspected, the Fund Development Committee may approve acceptance of the gift with no further environmental analysis required.

In all other cases, acceptance of gifts of real property shall require that a Phase I Environmental Site Assessment in compliance with the American Society for Testing and Materials (ASTM) Standard Practice be prepared by a competent environmental professional. The gift may be accepted by the Fund Development Committee if the assessment reveals no presence or likely presence of a hazardous substance. If the Phase I assessment indicates the presence or likely presence of a hazardous substance, NAME OF NONPROFIT may elect to obtain a Phase II assessment relative to the specific type of hazardous substance. If the Phase II assessment indicates that the property contains a hazardous substance, NAME OF NONPROFIT may accept the gift only upon the approval of the Fund Development Committee based upon advice of legal counsel concerning potential liability under CERCLA (Comprehensive Environmental Response, Compensation, and Liability Act of 1980) and other applicable laws.

C. Types of Planned Giving Vehicles

1. *Charitable Remainder Trusts.* Under a charitable remainder trust, the donor transfers assets to the trust in exchange for a life income. The donor may be the only income beneficiary, share the income with another, or gift the income to a third party. All charitable remainder trust documents shall be reviewed by the Executive Director or his/her designee prior to acceptance. NAME OF NONPROFIT will not serve as trustee of charitable remainder trusts but may recommend interested donors to independent legal or financial service companies with whom the donor can contract at his/her own expense and risk.

2. *Charitable Lead Trusts.* Under a Charitable Lead Trust, a donor transfers property to a trust and NAME OF NONPROFIT receives a specified payment for the term of the trust. When the trust terminates, the assets revert to the donor or pass to the donor's heirs. NAME OF NONPROFIT will not serve as trustee of charitable remainder trusts but will accept beneficiary status.

3. *Gift of a Personal Residence or Farm with a Retained Life Estate.* NAME OF NONPROFIT may accept a gift of a personal residence or farm with a life estate retained by the donor. The donor may retain the right to live in the property, share this right with another, or gift the right to a third party. Acceptance of the property shall be subject to all the requirements for the acceptance of any gift of real property. In addition, NAME OF NONPROFIT shall have a written agreement with the donor concerning maintenance, insurance, taxes, and other matters. At the death of the final life tenant, NAME OF NONPROFIT shall have unrestricted title to the property. Acceptance of a gift of a personal residence or a farm with a retained life estate shall require the prior approval of the Fund Development Committee.

4. *Gifts Posing Substantial Risk.* The Executive Director or his/her designee will seek the approval of the Fund Development Committee and the Board of Directors for acceptance of any gift which in their judgment poses substantial risk to NAME OF NONPROFIT, even if they are otherwise authorized by these Policies and Procedures to approve such gift.

D. Administration of Gifts

1. *Converting Gifts to Cash.* In general, NAME OF NONPROFIT's policy will be to immediately convert all received charitable gifts to cash, except when recommended otherwise by the Executive Director and approved by the Executive Committee.

2. *Use of Independent Legal and Financial Contractors.* It shall be NAME OF NONPROFIT's policy to recommend that prospective donors use independent legal and financial contractors in their estate or legacy planning.

3. *Designated or Restricted Gift.* NAME OF NONPROFIT reserves the right to refuse any designated or restricted gift

when the conditions placed on the acceptance of the gift are not in keeping with NAME OF NONPROFIT's mission and goals and/or would place an undue burden on the organization.

4. *Monitoring of Estates and Trusts.* All estates and trusts in which NAME OF NONPROFIT is a beneficiary shall be monitored by the Executive Director or his/her designee. Procedures shall include the acquisition and review of relevant court documents pertaining to each estate, calculation of approximate gift value, and periodic checks of the distribution process. NAME OF NONPROFIT may retain legal counsel, as appropriate, in estate proceedings.

5. *Avoidance of Trusteeship.* NAME OF NONPROFIT will not serve as the trustee for any type of charitable trust and instead, whenever possible, will recommend that all trusts of which NAME OF NONPROFIT is the beneficiary be managed by independent legal and financial contractors. Exceptions to this policy require the prior approval of Board of Directors and will be made in compliance with relevant state and federal laws.

6. *Endowment Funding.* As recommended by the Executive Director and with the prior approval of the Board of Directors, the proceeds from undesignated charitable gifts made through planned or legacy giving will be used in the establishment of an endowment fund to support NAME OF NONPROFIT's long-term mission and goals.

ACKNOWLEDGEMENT OF CONTRIBUTIONS

It is the policy of the organization to acknowledge all contributions made regardless of the amount of contribution. It will be the responsibility of the Executive Director to ensure that all contributions are acknowledged within 2 business days of receipt.

RESOURCE THREE

SAMPLE CONFIDENTIALITY POLICY

NAME OF NONPROFIT has an obligation to respect the privacy of its donors and to protect and maintain the confidentiality of all information it acquires concerning our them.

Confidentiality, for the purpose of this document, includes information that should be held in the strictest confidence and trust whether disclosed orally or in writing, to directors, volunteers, staff, donors, prospective donors, vendors or others holding a business relationship with NAME OF NONPROFIT.

With these principals in mind, NAME OF NONPROFIT has developed this "Confidentiality Policy" to more clearly define the scope and nature of confidential information.

I. CONFIDENTIALITY OF RECORDS

NAME OF NONPROFIT's Board and staff shall be responsible for maintaining the confidentiality of the records for donors and prospective donors. NONPROFIT NAME's staff may make all or part of any record available to Foundation volunteers to assist them in executing their specific responsibilities. NAME OF NONPROFIT's auditors, legal counsel and other contractors may be authorized to review donor/prospect and fund records as required for the purposes for which they are engaged.

All persons accessing donor/prospect records in the conduct of NAME OF NONPROFIT's business shall maintain the confidentiality of said records. Before any person may view a confidential record said person shall be provided with a copy of this policy and agree to follow it. Staff may share information with donors pertaining to their own gifts upon the donor's request.

II. PUBLICATION OF DONOR NAMES

Unless otherwise requested by the donor, the names of all individual donors may be printed in NAME OF NONPROFIT's annual report and in other appropriate listings or categories. NAME OF NONPROFIT will not publish the amount of any donor's gift without the permission of the donor. Unless otherwise specified in the document, donors making gifts to NAME OF NONPROFIT by bequest or other testamentary device are deemed to have granted such permission.

III. REMEMBRANCE GIFTS

The names of donors of memorial, honorarium or tribute gifts may be released to the honoree, next of kin, or appropriate member of the immediate family, unless otherwise specified by the donor. Gift amounts are not to be released without the express consent of the donor.

IV. ANONYMOUS GIFTS

NAME OF NONPROFIT is authorized to accept anonymous gifts. The name of the donor and size of the gift may be withheld from the Board of Directors if so requested by the donor. When made known to Board members, they will respect the anonymity of any such gift.

V. THIRD PARTY DISCLOSURES

NAME OF NONPROFIT shall not release to third parties or allow third parties to copy, inspect or otherwise use Foundation records or other information pertaining to a donor or donor's gifts. No disclosures to third parties of such information, including addresses and demographic information, shall be made without the donor's consent.

VII. PUBLIC DISCLOSURE

NAME OF NONPROFIT will comply with both the letter and spirit of all public disclosure requirements, including the open availability of its Form 990 tax returns and annual audit. This Confidentiality Policy shall not be construed in any manner to prevent the NAME OF NONPROFIT from disclosing information to taxing authorities or other governmental agencies or courts having regulatory control or jurisdiction over NAME OF NONPROFIT. However, all Board members, staff, volunteers, agents and contractors must hold strictly confidential all information of a private nature, including, but not limited to, all items explicitly discussed in this policy.

VIII. CONSEQUENCES OF POLICY VIOLATION

Violations of the Confidentiality Policy are considered serious, and may result in disciplinary action, up to and including dismissal for employees, agents or contractors, or removal from the Board of Directors or the separation of any volunteer from a committee or other representative role on behalf of NAME OF NONPROFIT. Violations of this policy are to be reported to the President of the Board.

By signing this document I acknowledge that I understand NAME OF NONPROFIT's confidentiality policies and agree to abide by them.
SIGNED: DATE:

ABOUT THE AUTHOR

Carl W. Davis is a Certified Fundraising Executive and graduate of The Salvation Army College for Officer Training in Chicago, Illinois. He has been a professional fundraiser for more than fifteen years having started his career as an Officer in The Salvation Army where he held the rank of Captain and served as an Executive Director. Carl also holds a Certificate in Fundraising Management from the Indiana University Lilly Family School of Philanthropy and has served as a Peer Mentor with the Chicago Chapter of the Association of Fundraising Professionals. Carl has served as the national Director of Development for a nation-wide civil rights advocacy nonprofit, the Development Director for a legal-aid nonprofit, the Director of Individual Giving for a Community and Economic Development Corporation and as a Major Gifts Officer for The Rotary Foundation of Rotary International. Carl enjoys working with nonprofit professionals and volunteer fundraisers by providing training in donor-centric fundraising philosophy and technique. He can be reached at carldaviscfre@gmail.com.

WITH THANKS:

I wish to extend sincere thanks and appreciation to the following individuals who generously provided their editing services for this book. Each of them contributed greatly and improved this book considerably. Any errors or mistakes that remain are my completely my own.

Brian J. Davis
Theodore Jackson, PhD
Melissa Kelsey
Michael S. Young, JD

I also wish to extend thanks to Laura Wolf for her creative and artistic assistance. As I have no skills in that area, her assistance was invaluable.

NOTES:

[i] M+R 2015 Benchmarks Report available at www.mrss.com

Names and other identifying information about donors or specific nonprofits have been changed to protect privacy.

Nothing in this book should be considered legal, tax or financial advice. All opinions expressed in this book belong to the author alone and do not necessarily reflect the opinions, policies or positions of any nonprofit for which the author has served as an employee, volunteer or consultant.

Made in the USA
Middletown, DE
18 March 2021